# The Roaring of the Lion

# The Roaring of the Lion

*A Commentary on Amos*

RAY BEELEY M.A.

RETIRED MINISTER OF RICHMOND WESLEYAN REFORM
CHURCH SHEFFIELD

THE BANNER OF TRUTH TRUST

THE BANNER OF TRUTH TRUST
3 Murrayfield Road, Edinburgh, EH12 6EL
PO Box 621, Carlisle, Pennsylvania 17013, USA

*

© 1969 Ray Beeley
First published 1970
Reprinted 1997

*

ISBN 0 85151 715 3

*

Printed in Finland by WSOY –
Book Printing Division

TO THE GLORY OF GOD
AND
TO THE MEMORY OF MY
FATHER IN WHOM I FIRST
SAW THE FRUIT OF GODLINESS

# CONTENTS

# PREFACE

For some years various members of my church and old scholars of my school have been urging me to collect a series of sermons together to publish a book, but this little volume has taken us all by surprise, and is quite different from what any of us would have planned.

It emerged from my re-starting a habit of my early Christian years and making notes from my own personal Bible study to clarify thoughts and help concentration – 'thoughts disentangle themselves when passing through lips or over pencil tips'. Before long these notes took a little more shape as some of my young people asked me to help them with their personal Bible study, and I duplicated notes on some of the Psalms. Eventually, I showed the Rev. Iain Murray a set of handwritten notes I had done on Amos and he encouraged me to put them down in order with the possibility of publication. I owe the Banner of Truth Trust a deep debt of gratitude for encouragement and many helpful suggestions. Others, too, deserve my thanks – the people from the school and the Church who typed, read and encouraged me, and my own family who bore with me whilst I worked at it.

Supremely, however, I thank God, for His Salvation, for His Son, my Saviour, for the grace of His Spirit to guide and uphold, and not least for this wonderful Book, the Holy Bible, which He caused to be written by His chosen men.

# 1: *The Background to the Prophecy*

## INTRODUCTION

Evangelical scholars generally regard Amos as one of the earliest of the great Hebrew writing prophets of the eighth century BC. Some point out the similarities which exist between Amos and Joel [*eg Joel* 3.18 and *Amos* 9.13] and accepting the priority of Joel, they argue that since the phrase 'The Lord shall roar out of Zion and utter his voice from Jerusalem' which opens the prophecy of Amos occurs also in *Joel* 3.16, this indicates that Amos was using this phrase from the earlier prophet as the starting point for his work. The prophecy of Amos was precisely dated, though we are not now able to fix it accurately. Chapter 1.1 mentions 'two years before the earthquake', which may well have been a great earthquake in the reign of Uzziah which was remembered with awe centuries later [see *Zech* 14.5].

## THE MAN

Amos was a herdsman and grower of sycomore fruit from Tekoa, in Southern Judah, a small town situated in the highlands about 5 miles South-East of Bethlehem. The area from which he came is described as 'wilderness' [*2 Chron* 20.20], so it may be assumed that he had a tough hard life and did not find it easy to obtain a living. He learned to endure hardness in God's training school – remember *Heb* 5.8 and 12.6. Here

[11]

we see the hand of God in providence, training His men long before they hear His call –cf Jer 1.5. Amos never had any formal education in the prophetic schools of his day as those which had gathered round Elijah and Elisha [Amos 7.14]. (The existence of these schools is reflected in 2 Kings 2.3, 5.7, 6.1–7). Yet he was no untutored rustic. He reveals a deep knowledge of history and of the problems of his day. In his prophecy there are many points of contact with the Pentateuch, for example:

Amos 2.7    Deut 23.17-18 – against religious prostitution.
Amos 2.8    Exod 22.26; Deut 24.12-13 – garments taken in pledge.
Amos 2.12   Num 6.1-21 – the consecration of the Nazarites.
Amos 4.4    Deut 14.28; 26.12 – tithing after three years.
Amos 4.5    Lev 2.11; 7.12 – the sacrifices of thanksgiving.

He uses the terms for sacrifice which are suggestive of intimate knowledge of the Pentateuch – 4.5, free-will offering; 5.21, solemn assembly; 5.22, meal offering, burnt offering and peace offering.

Thus we have a man prepared, equipped, disciplined and enabled by God to fulfil his calling and we may remember with gratitude that this is always so – His call is always based on exact knowledge and the sufficiency of His power to equip. We may follow through our Christian lives in the light of this conviction. If He calls, He will make us competent to the task. He will not hesitate to discipline and test. We must realize that the ability must come from Him and is not of ourselves [2 Cor 3.5]. Perhaps the hardest lesson we shall have to learn is that of dependence as, on occasion, He allows us to be reduced to helplessness, but He will enable us to do all that He intends. He means us to be 'more than conquerors' [Rom 8.37]. Furthermore it is worth noticing that a vital part of Amos' equipment was his deep knowledge of the Word of God as given up to that time. He knew it well and used it to interpret and answer the problems of his day. We should likewise study the Word of God diligently, store it in our minds and apply it to the situations of our day and age [Ps 119.11, 49-50; 2 Tim 2.15].

Amos heard the sovereign call of God as he was engaged in his ordinary occupation [7.14-15] and like the apostles in a later day, he left all and followed, conscious that even his response was peculiarly the work of God in his soul – 'The Lord took me'. He found himself engaged in a peculiarly difficult work – a Southerner ministering to the North, a countryman facing the sophistication of the nobility and a professional priesthood, a prophet of doom to an age which felt comfortable and secure in its materialism.

Here again we have lessons to learn if we would be acceptable servants of God:

1. *the duty of absolute obedience now!*
2. *the realization that whatever we are is by grace alone.*
3. *the assurance that by that same grace we can fulfil our calling.*

We may feel like *grasshoppers* [Num 13.33] but grace will make us competent [Num 14.7-9]. Faithfulness in present duties will open the door to wider callings. The call of God comes to the man who is diligently engaged in his present task [Exod 3.1-2; Judg 6.11-12; 1 Kings 19.19; Mark 1.16].

## HIS SITUATION
Amos exercised his ministry during the reigns of Uzziah in Judah and Jeroboam II in Israel. It was a kind of Indian Summer before the dreadful period of Assyrian invasion. In the kingdoms at the time there was peace, the apparent stability of long reigns, and great commercial wealth to which archaeology has borne its objective witness. In the South, Uzziah had strengthened his fortifications and built up his armies, successfully engaged the Philistines in the West, and recaptured the important port of Elath on the Red Sea from the Edomites. In the North Jeroboam II had followed the energetic action

of Jehoash in checking the growing Syrian power and had even occupied the Syrian capital city of Damascus, his most dangerous enemy. Considerable wealth accumulated from the spoils taken in battle, from the taxes and tolls which could be exacted when kingdoms so strategically placed on the Near Eastern trade routes were militarily strong; and from the oppression of the poorer classes by their richer neighbours which eventually brought many of the freemen to slavery.

Amos saw both the hazardous nature and the corrupting influence of this prosperity and it was his task to challenge it in a period of complacency, materialism and hardness of heart. Obviously this was a hard stand to take, yet he could not shirk the heavenly commission. Verses in Chapters 2 [14-16] and 3 [12] may well reflect this situation. The former make reference to the stalwart archers, the fleetfooted pursuers, and the excellent cavalry, yet speak of the way all this apparent strength will be brought low. The latter reflects how dreadful the overthrow will be. The people would be destroyed as sheep are devoured by a wolf or lion: all the shepherd would rescue would be two legs or the piece of an ear. The reference to the couch and the corner of a bed have been variously interpreted but almost certainly it is intended to give the impression of opulence and luxury suddenly and catastrophically destroyed. Like Amos we must not be taken in by illusions of worldly opulence and apparent security, nor may we shrink from our God-given duty to challenge man's connivance in his own deception, though there may be little sign of response.


HIS MESSAGE

The tone of the message of Amos is set right at the opening of the book, [1.1] where the earthquake is mentioned. The imagery here introduced runs throughout the book –see 5.8; 6.9, 11; 8.8; 9.1; 9.5.

It emphasizes:

1. The omnipotence of God who is able to shake the very fabric of the universe.
2. The temporary and dependent nature of the created universe upon which all men's wealth is founded.

At the outset, the power and judgement of the Almighty are brought into view – the Lord will roar as a lion from Jerusalem [1.2]. Throughout the book, except for a brief passage at the end, the message is one of doom. Jehovah is not to be thought of as an excuser of sin, an indulger of the follies of His own people. So we have the solemn warning of 5.18-20. The Hebrews tended to look to the Day of the Lord as the day of their glory and power, but Amos reminds them that in their unrepentant state it will be for them a day of darkness and not light, a day when sin will be called to account. The nature of their failure is clearly analysed in 5.21-27.

Here is warning against:

1. Materialism, and trust in human wisdom and strength – compare *Jer* 9.23-24; 17.5-6.
2. Complacency in sin – compare *Eccl* 8.11.
3. Irresponsible resting on privilege – compare *Luke* 3.8.

Yet again we are reminded how applicable is the message to our own day; we must not fear to speak of the awfulness of the judgement which must fall on the unrepentant sinner. The Lord is the God of righteousness who will not indulge sin but must pour upon it the inescapable vials of His wrath unless there is a true heartfelt repentance. This is the solemn message made necessary by the persistence of the chosen people in their sin. Even so the message of grace is not entirely absent since at the end of the book [9.11-15] there is anticipation of a day of joyful restoration; for as in the days of Noah, God is not without a faithful remnant in the midst of universal judgement. Even in the midst of judgement there is a clear call to repent [5.4, 14-15].

The message may be divided into two parts:

1-2.5 Denunciation of the nations surrounding Israel – Damascus, Gaza, Tyre, Edom, Ammon and Moab, and a short oracle upon Judah.

2.6-9.15 Concerned with Israel.

This may be regarded as a subtle device by the prophet to gain himself a hearing. He uses the denunciation pronounced upon the nations to excite the interest and attention of Israel; men start to listen when someone other than themselves is being denounced! The Lord reminded His disciples that they needed to be as wise as serpents. Could it be that we as Christians concern ourselves too little with seeking a contemporary presentation of our message, making pretended dependence on the Holy Spirit an excuse for mental laziness or lack of real concern?

## THE DOCTRINAL CONTENT

Though Amos is one of the earliest of the 'writing prophets' there is nothing immature about the doctrinal content of his message. To some, his message may appear to be overbalanced on the side of severity but this may be accounted for and defended by the task he had to fulfil. In many ways he was like John the Baptist, for his commission was to call a sin-deadened people to repentance and the first requirement was that they should see their need. The message of grace was not entirely absent, unless one descends to the unscrupulous and unjustifiable expedient of cutting off the final section of the prophecy, but the exposition of it was to be committed to Amos' slightly younger contemporary, Hosea.

[a] Doctrine of God

1. The Creator of the universe. 5.8.
2. His transcendence and omniscience. 9.1-4.
3. His special choice of the Hebrews. 3.2-3.

[16]

4. His emphasis on social righteousness. 5.24.
5. God as the Lord of History. 1.-2. 5.
6. His refusal of empty formal religion. 5.21-23.
7. The promise of the preservation and restoration of a remnant. 9.9-11.

[b] Failure of man
  1. Man's failure to listen to God. 2.4; 4.11; 7.12-13, 16.
  2. His wrong view of 'religion'. 5.4-5, 21-26.
  3. The selfish luxury of the upper classes. 3.15; 6.4-6.
  4. The insatiable greed of the merchants. 8.5-6.
  5. The covetous landowners. 2.7; 3.10; 5.11.
  6. The perversion of justice. 5.12.

[c] Religious failure
  1. The multiplication of sacrifice and ritual: 4.4-5; 5.21-23.
  2. The religious prostitution. 2.7.
  3. The drunken orgies: 2.8 (Amos does not actually mention drunken orgies but *Hosea* 7.5-6 indicates that drunken orgies were common enough at court).
  4. The blind sense of security: 5.18.

The special emphasis here is on righteousness in the sense of God's expectation of right behaviour, His just demands upon men as responsible moral beings. This applies to all, whether Jew or Gentile. Each will be judged according to light received. Man must see his need and repent. [5.4-6, 14-15].

# 2: Review of the Prophecy

## THE ORACLES AGAINST THE NATIONS
It is made clear that the Lord is the Judge of all. The nations are all responsible before Him and the sins indictable are those of which they are aware; God does not judge men by standards which they do not know [*Rom* 1.32]. The contemporary importance of this is, that to say, 'I do not believe in God', does not excuse me from the bar of His judgement. If I am prepared to be honest I have to admit that I have come short even of the imperfect and incomplete standard which I know. Man knows himself to be without excuse [*Rom* 1.20].

## THE DENUNCIATION OF ISRAEL
This is summarized in 3.2-3. The unique privilege of Israel involves them also in increased responsibility.

1. *The privilege of undeserved love* – '*You only have I known.*'
2. *The pattern of united living* – '*Can two walk together except they be agreed?*'
3. *The punishment of uncontrolled licence* –'*Therefore will I punish you for all your iniquities.*'

1. Israel has been brought into a unique relationship of intimacy with God. The word 'known' is often used of the relationship between husband and wife. The Church is the Bride of Christ. This relationship is born of sovereign love.

2. Because of this relationship they must walk with God; they must be agreed.

The Lord had made this clear to them in many different ways [2.11]. He had given them prophets to whom He had revealed His secrets [3.7].

He had borne with their sin for a long time [2.13].

He had warned them of what would happen. They had been forewarned of the coming judgement [3.13-15].

The rod of correction had been applied to call them to repentance before it was too late:

Chapter 4 *V*6 – Famine.
        *V*7 – Drought.
        *V*9 – Pestilence.
        *V*10 – Defeat and slaughter in battle.
        *V*11 – Earthquake or some other terrible providential disaster.

Since these had not had the desired effect there would be a final assize:

*V*12 – PREPARE TO MEET THY GOD –
but even in judgement He was still their God.

3. They had walked in perverseness and their sins were against the light. They were under the cover of professed allegiance and therefore under the curse of an empty religion which did not transform the soul and fit it to walk with God. The prophet not only condemns the falseness of the worship they were offering but points out the moral shortcomings which accompanied it.

Chapter 2 *V*6 – Bribery; also mentioned 5.7, 10, 12.
        *V*6-7 – Greed, oppression and immorality, 5.11; see also 8.4-6.
Chapter 4 *V*1 – The laziness, heartlessness and self-indulgence of the women.
Chapter 6 *V*4-6 – Luxury, gluttony, drunkenness.

# THE JUDGEMENT OF GOD

The judgement of God is declared in five prophetic visions:

1. *The vision of a locust plague:* God promises He will withdraw the plague after the intercession of the prophet [7.1-3]. The Authorised Version speaks of 'grasshoppers' – modern versions generally agree that locusts are intended.

2. *The vision of a consuming fire:* once again the threat is withdrawn after the intercession of the prophet [7.4-6].

3. *The vision of the plumbline:* God's measuring of the city symbolizes the Divine searching out of the nation, which is weighed, measured and found wanting [7.7-11].

4. *The vision of the fruit basket:* emphasizing the imminence of the threatened judgement [8.1-3].

5. *The vision of the altar:* making the final indictment of an empty religion. The doom is now inescapable [9.1-4].

The following lessons may be deduced from this vision of judgement:

(i) The patience of God. In response to the prayer of the prophet, the judgement, so richly deserved, is twice delayed.

(ii) The importance of intercession. Intercession may result in repentance; at the very least it gives men time to hear and answer the Divine call.

(iii) The carefulness of God. His judgement is never hasty. The city was measured before it was judged – compare the situation before the Flood [*Gen* 6] and before God destroyed Sodom and Gomorrah [*Gen* 18.20-21].

(iv) The imminence of the judgement. Apart from repentance, following upon divine grace and mercy, judgement is inescapable.


# THE WAY OF REPENTANCE

5.4-6. These verses put the demand personally. It is not enough to go to the place of worship or to seek the forms of religion;

we need to meet God. The prophet reminds the people of the solemn nature of this meeting, for unless there is repentance 'He will break forth as a fire'. They need to recapture the solemn realization of His holiness which their fore-fathers had when the Lord appeared to them from the top of Mount Sinai [*Exod* 19].

5.14-15. Here Amos speaks of the practical consequences. When a man repents there is a change of heart, a new line of action, uprightness of life, love of that which is good. These are the evidences God seeks [compare the preaching of John the Baptist in *Luke* 3.8-14].

5.21-24. Amos draws the contrast between empty formalism and the evidence of life-giving truth. Here is the essential message of the eighth-century prophet in a nutshell, a warning against the kind of religion which is mere form and does not change the life [*cf Is* 1.10-18: *Hos* 6.6; *Mic* 6.6-8].

## THE PROMISE OF FUTURE RESTORATION [9.11-15]

Many scholars have tried to deny the genuineness of this oracle simply because it does have this note of hope, but to do this is to miss the whole genius of Divine revelation, that the Lord in sovereign grace has decreed the salvation of a remnant, in spite of all that human sin and folly can do – He will not finally cast off His people whom he foreknew [*Rom* 11.2]. After all the sifting [*Amos* 9.9] a remnant will finally be saved to glorify God.

The New Testament sets its seal to the authenticity of this passage, for James quotes from it in the great Council at Jerusalem [*Acts* 15.16-17] seeing verse 11 as fulfilled in Christ. The believer in Old or New Testament alike is a child of *hope*!

## THE RELEVANCE OF THE PROPHECY TO THE PRESENT DAY

Before we proceed to attempt an exposition of the text, this would seem to be the place for an assessment of the particular application and relevance of the prophecy.

1. *The Judgement of God* is presented as an inescapable fact; Jehovah is the Sovereign Lord of History and Creation and all men are answerable to Him. His own people are reminded that they are responsible in a special way [3.2-3]. God is seen as infinitely patient but He will not restrain His wrath for ever, because He is also infinitely just, and there must come a precise inescapable rendering of account.

2. *The failure of Man*
[a] The danger of a paganized religion – there are three aspects particularly noted by Amos.
  (i) Emphasis on forms and places.
  (ii) Danger of 'syncretism' – based upon a borrowing from other religions and the acceptance of their standards, unacceptable to God.
  (iii) Failure to shoulder social responsibilities.
[b] The strength of the desires of the flesh.
  (i) Luxury.
  (ii) Gluttony and drunkenness.
  (iii) Immorality – sexual standards of a pagan world accepted.
  (iv) Oppression and dishonesty – the result of the policy of 'anything goes' to get rich quickly.
[c] The debasement of moral conscience.
  (i) Despising the Law of God.
  (ii) Perverting the righteous and seeking to silence the prophets.

Each of these finds its counterpart in our twentieth-century world:
[a] In many parts of Christendom the forms and ceremonies are scrupulously maintained, with an increasing emphasis upon ritual, while at the same time there is a growing abandonment of scriptural doctrines and biblical standards

of morality, even by so-called church leaders. In the last few years almost every major New Testament doctrine has been called in question, in an attempt to gain an imagined intellectual respectability. At the same time the Christian Church has failed, all too often, to think or speak clearly and act decisively in social matters such as marriage and divorce, crime and punishment, care of the aged, education of children, racialism, poverty and famine; and worse still, the individual believer has often seemed to behave without conviction in these matters.

[b] The rising standard of living has drawn many Christians into the whirlpool of 'keeping up with the Joneses' and a consequent decline in the sense of stewardship. We live as though life owed us every kind of labour-saving device and plenty of money for leisure, pleasure and self-indulgence. In England there is a general neglect of Christian standards of honesty, integrity and purity as the 'permissive society' has been allowed to take over.

[c] Many Christian teachers and preachers are aggrieved by the hardness of heart and indifference to spiritual and moral issues which they meet on all sides where many have given themselves up to the satisfaction of their physical appetites.

3. *The Grace of God*
The nature of His love and grace is seen in that:

[a] He continues to send the prophets although they are not heeded.

[b] He restrains the judgement so richly deserved and perseveres instead in warnings.

[c] He continues to call to repentance a nation which had already demonstrated itself fit only to be judged.

[d] He promises the restoration of a remnant of a nation which deserved only to be cast off.

So today, for all the moral decline in our land, God has not left Himself without witnesses and there are many, perhaps particularly amongst young people, who know His grace and are eager to bear their witness by word and action.

## 4. The Difficulty of the Witness

Amos was called to a hard task. He had to minister in a strange place to difficult people, already far gone in the paths of sin. They did not want to hear. They ridiculed what he had to say. His message was grim and threatening in an age which cried out for excitement and heady wine. He was lonely; few would listen and fewer still would lend support. He had no professional qualifications and had to challenge the officers of government, the nobility and the official priestly caste. He must depend on the grace of God alone.

At these four points the Book of Amos seems particularly relevant to our day and age. He spoke to a people who were self-sufficient in the extreme because of a temporary material prosperity which had completely blinded them to the realities of the situation. Their arrogance in success had caused them to be unmindful of the precariousness of their political and economic prosperity. They were disregarding their essential insufficiency to stand alone in a world where they were enjoying temporary benefit from the embarrassments of their more powerful neighbours. Like twentieth-century man in the presence of the threat of nuclear war and the creeping moral paralysis threatening his society, their optimistic irresponsibility bore an air of unreality and self-deception. The prophet was not only speaking spiritual truth in his denunciations, they also bore the stamp of down-to-earth practicality. Israel needed God; they needed a miracle! Politically and militarily they did not have the strength to withstand the pressure of their powerful imperial neighbours. Socially the policies which led to the consolidation of wealth in the hands of a few, whilst condemning the majority of the freemen first to poverty then to slavery, were bound to lower the morale and ultimately undermine the stability of the nation.

The prophet's discernment of the situation went even deeper. He saw that the real danger was spiritual: he saw things not from the earthly viewpoint of an astute politician but from the standpoint of eternity. Inevitably in such a man-centred society the concepts of Divine judgement and human accountability had been ignored, bringing the inevitable fruit of individual degeneration and social disintegration. Amos exposes these errors, reminding his hearers of the Divine sovereignty and the inescapable reality of the Divine judgement. In challenging words he assures them that the only deliverance from the imminent ruin to which they are heading must come through grace and mercy to be received through sincere repentance.

Finally we have a message to the professedly religious which also has a contemporary ring – 'Can two walk together except they be agreed?' True religion is in the realm of personal communion and moral obedience; anything less is false show.

The experience of Amos reminds us that the messenger of such tidings must be very sure that he has been sent by God, and that he is fulfilling his commission in dependence upon the all-sufficiency of the Divine resources. No other foundation will guarantee his perseverance. God's messengers must expect to tread a lonely and rejected path. They may well find that they are nobody's darling and everybody's butt, so it would be well for them at the outset to be prepared to be regarded as the 'offscouring of all things' [1 Cor 4.13]. We have the warning of Jesus, 'Woe unto you when all men speak well of you, for so did the fathers to the false prophets' [Luke 6.26].

# 3: *Opening Oracles against the nations of Israel and Judah*

INTRODUCTION

Chapter 1 *V*1-2

1 The words of Amos, who was among the herdmen of Tekoa, which he saw concerning Israel in the days of Uzziah king of Judah, and in the days of Jeroboam the son of Joash king of Israel, two years before the earthquake.

2 And he said, The Lord will roar from Zion, and utter his voice from Jerusalem; and the habitations of the shepherds shall mourn, and the top of Carmel shall wither.

*V*1: **A herdman.** Amos was a humble nobody. He was not one of the trained religious. He spoke by revelation, not by human wisdom. When we speak as Christians, do we have the personal conviction of 'a man sent from God'? or do we merely speak words which we have learned by heart or picked up from books?

**Tekoa.** A wilderness area in the dry and sandy South of Judah where it would be no easy matter to earn a living. Many a man of God has been trained for God in the midst of hard providences, as was Joseph in the land of Egypt. The disciple must learn to accept discipline [*Heb* 10.36; 12.6; 1 *Pet* 1.6-7; 5.10].

It is worth noting how many of the great men of the Old

Testament were herdmen or shepherds – Abraham, Jacob, Moses, David. The occupation suggests certain characteristics required in the useful man of God:

1. Patience to keep at a routine job day after day.
2. Watchfulness lest any of the flock go astray or intruders seek to kill or steal.
3. Discipline against self-indulgence which might slacken watchfulness.
4. Steadfastness born of reliance on God to face loneliness and danger without fear.
5. Devotion to duty for seeking the lost which may prove a painful and tedious task requiring unremitting application.
6. Courage to face marauders or wild animals. It was as a shepherd that David faced the lion and the bear.

The Lord Jesus Christ gloried in the title of the 'Good Shepherd' and He calls some to be under-shepherds [*John* 21.15-17; 1 *Pet* 5.1-2]. The above are certainly characteristics to be cultivated by the Christian – a part of the equipment with which the Holy Spirit endues the believer, to be worked out in conscious remembrance of *Phil* 2.13.

**Uzziah, Jeroboam.** Uzziah was king in Judah, Jeroboam in the Northern Kingdom of Israel. Both had long and materially prosperous reigns.
During this period:

1. There was abundant wealth in Israel but no gratitude of heart and no sense of responsibility to the Giver.
2. The material prosperity helped the nation on its downward path. The call to repentance had no urgency in the eyes of the majority [*Eccles* 8.11].

We are reminded of how we need to watch ourselves in prosperous days [*Mark* 10.23, 25].

**Two years before the earthquake.** This does not help us to fix the exact date of the prophecy, but plainly this disaster was still something of a landmark in history some three centuries later [*Zech* 14.5]. The imagery persists throughout the book [5.8; 6.9; 11; 8.8; 9.1; 9.5] and is employed in *Haggai* 2.6 as symbolic of God acting in judgement. It is vivid and valuable, reminding us of the overwhelming power of God and the essential insecurity of the material world in which we live. There is no earthly home of refuge from the day of Divine wrath – see *Ps* 46 by way of contrast.

*V*2: **The Lord will roar** [roars: RSV]. God warns before He acts in judgement, but when He **roars** like a ferocious lion, it is no empty threat – the most fertile areas will be utterly blasted and withered. The judgement threatened by God constitutes the most solemn call to repentance [*Luke* 13.3, 5; *Acts* 17.31; *Rom* 2.4-5].

**The Lord.** The Covenant name of God is employed here, from which we learn:

1. His judgements are in the interest of His people [*cf. Is* 43.3] The downfall of the heathen nations is in some way connected with the deliverance of Israel. Salvation and judgement may be two sides of the same act, as in the case of the Flood which was an act of judgement upon the godless and a deliverance for the family of Noah, God's elect remnant.
2. He is the **living God** – the '**I am**' – the God known by His actions.
3. His faithfulness, whether in love or judgement.
4. The God of creation and history is the Lord. He is working out his purposes of redemption in all history, which is His Story, a narrative of the triumph of redeeming love.

**From Zion.** Jerusalem was the place where God revealed himself and from where he reigned, not Samaria, the capital of the apostate northern kingdom. Zion was the 'Sun' round which the solar system of His purposes revolves. His people are the centre of His purposes because they are hidden 'in Christ' and He is pre-eminent in all things [Eph 1.20-23; Col 1.18].

**Habitations of shepherds: Mount Carmel.** Both are symbols of fertility and fruitfulness but perhaps there is also in mind the concept of universality – south – **Tekoa**, the habitation of shepherds; and north – **Carmel.** The judgement when it falls will be universal and devastating. Where men turn away from God and reject His grace, the result is inevitable barrenness – see *Jer* 17.5-6; and contrast *Jer* 17.7-8 and *Is* 3.5.

FOR MEDITATION

1. The Lord as Sovereign and Almighty. The stability of our Universe depends on His goodness and forbearance and longsuffering. When He speaks in judgement nothing can resist [*Hag* 2.6; 2 *Peter* 3.10-11] and speak in judgement He assuredly will. Both Christian and un-believer are answerable to God. [*Rom* 14.12; *Heb* 9.27].
2. The intimate relationship between the Lord and His people. They are at the very centre of His purposes. What manner of people ought we to be in view of this? [*1John* 3.1-3].
3. God's men are of necessity humble men, perhaps not even possessed of great natural gifts, but disciplined men, bred in the school of reality, not in the realm of philosophical speculation. God can take a shepherd from the wilderness of Tekoa and make him a prophet in Samaria. Answer the question found in *Jer* 32.27 and then ask God what He requires of you.
4. Consider what the latter part of verse 2 implies are the consequences of forsaking God – emptiness, barrenness, unquenched thirst. See *Ps* 63.1 and make it your prayer.

DENUNCIATION OF AND JUDGEMENT
UPON THE NATIONS
Chapter 1 *V*3-5

**3 Thus saith the Lord; For three transgressions of Damascus, and for four, I will not turn away the punishment thereof; because they have threshed Gilead with threshing instruments of iron:**

[29]

4 But I will send a fire into the house of Hazael, which shall devour the palaces of Benhadad.

5 I will break also the bar of Damascus, and cut off the inhabitant from the plain of Aven, and him that holdeth the sceptre from the house of Eden: and the people of Syria shall go into captivity unto Kir, saith the Lord.

### JUDGEMENT UPON DAMASCUS

*V*3: **For three transgressions and for four.** That is to say, for repeated and aggravated transgression. The particular crime condemned – **they threshed Gilead** – is that of utter brutality, which had been foretold in 2 *Kings* 8.12. Hazael had conquered Gilead [2 *Kings* 10.32*ff*]. He had indeed been used by God as a rod of chastening but had gone far beyond what was necessary even in war.

*V*4: The Lord would send judgement upon Hazael. All men are held responsible at the judgement bar of God.

**Ben Hadad** was a common name for Syrian kings: three are mentioned in the First and Second Book of Kings [1 *Kings* 15.18; 2 *Kings* 8.7; 13.3]. Ben Hadad was the name of the king killed by Hazael when he seized the throne. The story is told in 2 *Kings* 8.7-15.

*V*5: **Unto Kir.** The prophet here specifies that the judgement will come by the hand of Assyria.

**The bar** – the bar of the city gate.

**The plain of Aven** – a broad fertile valley in Lebanon. Aven, according to the Hebrew, may mean 'vanity' and refer to the idols of Syria. 1 *Kings* 20.23 may reflect the fact that Israel chose high places for her sanctuaries while the Syrians erected their altars in the valleys. This valley of Aven may have been a particular centre of Syrian idol worship.

**Beth-Eden** – a Syrian city. Matthew Poole suggests that the name 'house of pleasures' indicates a royal summer palace.

Here we see the special divinely-given insight of the prophet for at the time of the prophecy Assyria was in a state of weakness. In 2 *Kings* 16.9 we learn that the prophecy was exactly fulfilled. Kir was the place of origin of the Syrians [*Amos* 9.7]. To it they returned as captives. Its location is uncertain but it may have been near Elam, East of Babylon [*cf Is* 22.6].

Chapter 1 *V*6-8

6 **Thus saith the Lord; For three transgressions of Gaza, and for four, I will not turn away the punishment thereof; because they carried away captive the whole captivity, to deliver them up to Edom:**

7 **But I will send a fire on the wall of Gaza, which shall devour the palaces thereof:**

8 **And I will cut off the inhabitant from Ashdod, and him that holdeth the sceptre from Ashkelon, and I will turn mine hand against Ekron: and the remnant of the Philistines shall perish, saith the Lord God.**

JUDGEMENT UPON THE PHILISTINES

Gaza was the principal city of the Philistines and here stands representative for the whole Philistine people.

One of the incidents here spoken of as the transgressions of Gaza may well be that recorded in 2 *Chron* 21.16-17. The judgement upon Philistia is re-echoed in *Jer* 47.1-7; *Ezek* 25.15-17; *Zeph* 2.4-7; *Zech* 9.5-7.

The handing over of the Jews to Edom is seen as a particularly reprehensible crime since the Edomites were known to be the inveterate enemies of the Jews. Once again the crime is one of inhumanity. Even a nation outside the law of Moses is here held accountable to a law written upon man's conscience. In days when the godless seem in so many ways 'to get away with it', we need to remember that God does not forget and that His judgement is completely just. He requires that which is past [*Eccles* 3.15] even though it may have faded from man's memory.

[31]

9 Thus saith the Lord; For three transgressions of Tyrus, and for four, I will not turn away the punishment thereof; because they delivered up the whole captivity to Edom, and remembered not the brotherly covenant:

10 But I will send a fire on the wall of Tyrus, which shall devour the palaces thereof.

## JUDGEMENT UPON TYRE

*V*9: The brotherly covenant here mentioned may well be that between Hiram and Solomon which consolidated a friendship opened up by David [see 1 *Kings* 5]. Tyre at this later date joined in the brutal subjugation of Israel and became party to the crime of the Philistines previously mentioned. An old friendship had been forgotten [contrast 2 *Sam* 9, the story of David's kindness to Mephibosheth]. Here again we see God judging a heathen people on a universal law of conscience apart from the specific revelation of Law. 'For old time's sake' is not just an expression of outdated sentimentality but a principle of conscience which should commend itself to all men, an attitude of thankful remembrance of fellowship enjoyed.

*V*10: Nebuchadnezzar conducted a long siege of Tyre, some two hundred years later, when fiery missiles were extensively employed against the seemingly impregnable stronghold. The city does not appear to have been completely overthrown until the time of Alexander the Great. It was later rebuilt but reduced to rubble by the Saracens. Chapters 26, 27 and 28 of Ezekiel speak of Tyre's greatness and subsequent desolation. The eventual fate of Tyre is an important subject to remember in days when the proud and ungodly seem to be flourishing like a green bay tree [*Ps* 37.35-36]. The judgements of God may sometimes excite our impatience but viewed from the standpoint of the Word of God they are true and righteous altogether [*Ps* 19.9]. God delays their execution in order to give men time to repent, but when men continue in their sins the threatened evil eventually falls. As men sow, they reap! [*cf Joel* 3.4-8].

Chapter 1 *V*11-12

**11 Thus saith the Lord; For three transgressions of Edom, and for four, I will not turn away the punishment thereof; because he did pursue his brother with the sword, and did cast off all pity, and his anger did tear perpetually, and he kept his wrath for ever:**

**12 But I will send a fire upon Teman, which shall devour the palaces of Bozrah.**

JUDGEMENT UPON EDOM

The Edomites were descended from Esau and there should have been peace between Israel and Edom on the basis of the reconciliation of the brethren [*Gen* 33.4]. The Edomites became famed for their brutality which seems to have been unleashed in a particular way against Israel.

The offence of Edom may be summarized as 'unbrotherly conduct' – uncontrolled anger, bitterness, and a vengeful spirit. The brief but pointed prophecy of Obadiah sets out the situation and the judgement very vividly.

*V*12: **Teman** – a tribe reputed to be descended from Esau, or a city of northern Edom, 5 miles from Petra the capital of Edom which is not mentioned since it had already been devastated [2 *Kings* 14.7]. As a wall is not mentioned here (contrast Gaza, Tyre and Rabbah) it is more probable that a tribal country not a town is intended.

**Bozrah** – an Edomite city of some importance.

Chapter 1 *V*13-15

**13 Thus saith the Lord; For three transgressions of the children of Ammon, and for four, I will not turn away the punishment thereof; because they have ripped up**

[33]

the women with child of Gilead, that they might enlarge their border:

14 But I will kindle a fire in the wall of Rabbah, and it shall devour the palaces thereof, with shouting in the day of battle, with a tempest in the day of the whirlwind:

15 And their king shall go into captivity, he and his princes together, saith the Lord.

JUDGEMENT UPON AMMON (and Moab in 2.1):

The particular sin of the Ammonites was that of gross brutality when they were so set on acquiring additional territory that they became quite insensitive to any finer feelings. Ammon and Moab originated from the incestuous relationship between Lot and his two daughters (*Gen* 19.30-38). It may be noted that the religion of Lot did not have much effect on his progeny.

*V*14: **Rabbah.** The capital of Ammon.

According to Poole the judgement here spoken of was eventually completed by the Babylonians. Compare also *Ezek* 25.1-3

*V*15: **Their king.** This may signify the idol of the Ammonites as well as their king.

Chapter 2 *V*1-3

1 Thus saith the Lord; For three transgressions of Moab, and for four, I will not turn away the punishment thereof; because he burned the bones of the king of Edom into lime:

2 But I will send a fire upon Moab, and it shall devour the palaces of Kirioth: and Moab shall die with tumult, with shouting, and with the sound of the trumpet:

3 And I will cut off the judge from the midst thereof, and will slay all the princes thereof with him, saith the Lord.

[34]

God is concerned not only with the physical aspect of man but with the respect and dignity of man as a human being. The body, even when dead, is worthy of respect as the dwelling place of the soul during its earthly pilgrimage.

The particular crime dealt with here is not against the Israelites, God's chosen people, but against one of their inveterate enemies; even so, in the sight of God he has dignity as a human being. We need to remember that all men bear something of the image of God, no matter how much they have been degraded or even have degraded themselves. That image, however defaced, ought to command and receive respect. The concept of the dignity of the human body needs to be remembered today in relation to recent developments in medical science and the disposal of corpses. The fact that the Christian's body is the temple of the Holy Spirit [1 Cor 6.19] and is to be raised to immortality should lead us to treat it with respect.

V2: **Kirioth** was the capital city of Moab. It is referred to in Jeremiah 48, verse 24.

V3: The leaders of the nation are especially held responsible. Leadership in any sphere carries special responsibility to God.

*

Thus closes the section particularly concerned with the nations surrounding Israel. Maybe the prophet is using these denunciations to gain the ear of his own people who had become so dull of hearing. From this point he turns his attention to *Judah* [2.4-5] and then more largely to Israel itself.

FOR MEDITATION

1. The unusual and oblique way of approach the prophet employs of gaining an ear by denouncing the sins of the heathen reminds us that Christians need to be wise as serpents as well as harmless as doves. 'By all means save some' says Paul [1 Cor 9.22]. Are we as

thoughtful as we should be in finding a medium which will help us to communicate? Paul would not modify the Gospel but he would discover and employ any suitable way of approach.

2. We are reminded of the universal law of conscience written in the heart of every man. The godless nations are to be held responsible for their misdeeds. God has written an indelible testimony on their hearts. Hard though a man may be, he is not a stone! Though he may not like it, his conscience, though muffled, witnesses against him.

3. There is here a continuous demand for self-control, and respect for other human beings.

4. There is also a saddening picture of the way the human heart can be perverted[Jer 17.9], leading men to treat their fellow-beings in such an inhuman way as Amos denounces here. As in the case of Ammon [1.13-15] men can be so corrupted by the prospect of material gain that women with child fall victims to their insatiable lust and greed.

5. The reality of the judgement to come. All men and nations are held responsible to God. The Lord does not forget sin, save as it is laid on Christ. Christ alone is the ground of such promises as Jer 31.34 and Micah 7.18-19.

6. The Lord's special concern with His own people. Though He allows them to be chastened by the hands of men, His eye is still upon them. When his work of chastisement has been completed he will vindicate them, and, in due time, He will bring their enemies to judgement.

7. The dignity of man as a human being and of the body as the dwelling place of the soul. Man is essentially a spiritual being originally created in the image of God and is always to be treated as such. While we hate sin and ignorance we must not despise the man who is in bondage to them.

8. The importance of loyalty in human society. Breaking one's word to men, like breaking vows made to God, is a dreadful sin.

9. The supreme lesson is that of the sovereignty of God in history and providence. He is the Lord: His purposes are being worked out: the nations are all in His hand. In viewing the wide sweep of history we must never forget that His purposes are to be accomplished through His people who often seem to be a despised and neglected remnant, but one day will be vindicated and glorified.

[36]

4 Thus saith the Lord; For three transgressions of Judah, and for four, I will not turn away the punishment thereof; because they have despised the law of the Lord, and have not kept his commandments, and their lies caused them to err, after the which their fathers have walked:

5 But I will send a fire upon Judah, and it shall devour the palaces of Jerusalem.

### JUDGEMENT UPON JUDAH

The main crime of Judah is that of despising the Law of God, that of turning away from the Divine revelation. The privilege of the availability of the Word increases responsibility.

*V*4: **They have despised the law** – they have not regarded it with due reverence as the Word of God. They have cheapened it by lack of respect. When believers do not practise the Law of God they are despising it. They cause the Gospel to be blasphemed.

RV translates – **They have rejected**, as in 1 *Sam* 15.23, 26, with emphasis on the idea of wilful turning away in self-indulgence.

**And have not kept his commandments** – they have not obeyed its injunctions.

**Their lies** – false gods, false prophets, misplaced hopes. Many ways which seem right to a man [*Prov* 14.12] may prove lies in the sense that they promise much but do not satisfy and 'the end thereof are the ways of death'. We too may live 'under a lie' – whether that of the drug addict, the materialist, the humanist, or even a religious system; Each puts a mistaken 'Sun' at the centre of his system. The 'lie' may be quite a respectable sort of 'god' but it leads only to disappointed hopes in the present and ultimate destruction in the future. Notice

[37]

how men are held responsible for following false teachers. We are ordered to 'try the spirits' [1 *John* 4.1]. Man is not left without landmarks by which to judge his course. The tragedy of much of the philosophy and religion of our day is that it is removing the ancient landmarks [*Prov* 22.28]. Not that ancient things are sacrosanct in themselves, but these particular ancient landmarks were given and authenticated by God!

Chapter 2 *V*6-16

6 Thus saith the Lord; For three transgressions of Israel, and for four, I will not turn away the punishment thereof; because they sold the righteous for silver, and the poor for a pair of shoes;

7 That pant after the dust of the earth on the head of the poor, and turn aside the way of the meek: and a man and his father will go in unto the same maid to profane my holy name:

8 And they lay themselves down upon clothes laid to pledge by every altar, and they drink the wine of the condemned in the house of their God.

9 Yet destroyed I the Amorites before them, whose height was like the height of the cedars, and he was strong as the oaks; yet I destroyed his fruit from above, and his roots from beneath.

10 Also I brought you up from the land of Egypt, and led you forty years through the wilderness, to possess the land of the Amorite.

11 And I raised up of your sons for prophets, and of your young men for Nazarites. Is it not even thus, O ye children of Israel? saith the Lord.

12 But ye gave the Nazarites wine to drink; and commanded the prophets, saying, Prophesy not.

13 Behold, I am pressed under you, as a cart is pressed that is full of sheaves.

14 Therefore the flight shall perish from the swift, and

the strong shall not strengthen his force, neither shall
the mighty deliver himself:

15 Neither shall he stand that handleth the bow; and he
that is swift of foot shall not deliver himself: neither
shall he that rideth the horse deliver himself.

16 And he that is courageous among the mighty shall
flee away naked in that day, saith the Lord.

JUDGEMENT UPON ISRAEL

Here are two aspects of Israel's sin:

1. That resulting from a self-centred materialism which is not
   outwardly brutal but which is no less cruel because it is
   more refined.
2. That resulting from wrongheadedness in the realm of
   religion, issuing in the failure to comprehend the love and
   righteousness of God.

Instead of a personal relationship with God which expresses
itself in just and merciful dealings with our fellow-men,
religion becomes a dead routine of religious observance
without moral implications.

*V*6-8: SUMMARIZE THE NATURE OF ISRAEL'S SINS

*V*6: **They sold the righteous for silver** – a description of
corrupt judges who were willing to pervert justice for a bribe.
The parable of the Unjust Judge [*Luke* 18.1-8] reflects this
situation.

**The poor for a pair of shoes** – refers to the selling into
slavery of those who cannot pay the debts incurred at the
hands of greedy landlords. Both sins are the expression of the
heartlessness of a corrupt materialism and a society where
men are consumed with greed.

*V*7: **That pant after the dust . . .** There are two main
possibilities here:

1. Certain men are so greedy that they would even steal the

[39]

dust off the head of the poor man who has put on the traditional sack-cloth and ashes to bemoan his fate. Or,

2. They trample the poor man in the dust and kick the humble out of the way. They are utterly careless of the feelings of others. They set out to pervert the way of the meek who truly trust in God.

**A man and his father . . .** The reference here is probably to ceremonial prostitution. Sexual immorality and false religion are continually linked in the Bible. A low view of womanhood is related to a low view of God, a situation hinted at in the 'curse' of *Gen* 3.16. It is only when men and women are reconciled to God that they truly appreciate the sanctity of sex. The relationship between man and wife portrayed in *Eph* 5.22-33 is based on the Christian experience of reconciliation.

*V*8: **They lay themselves down . . .** A further indictment of cruel and heartless oppression, forbidden by the legislation of *Deut* 24.12-13. God expects His people to be merciful in their dealings with one another [*Matt* 5.7]. Justice is always to be tempered by mercy.

**They drink . . .** There are two possible interpretations:

1. *Living Prophecies* suggests, 'In my temple they offer wine purchased with stolen money'. Matthew Poole favours this interpretation.

2. They are drunk in their heathen orgies with wine paid for by their cruel oppressions. Oppression and self-indulgence go together!

*V*9-12: DEMONSTRATE HOW THIS WAS A GRIEVOUS
       ABUSE OF GRACE

*V*9: They are reminded of the mercy of God in overthrowing their enemies who could have kept them from enjoying the rich benefits of the land of promise, an incident described in *Num* 21.21-25. See also *Josh* 24.8

*V*10: Redeemed from the land of Egypt, guided through the

wilderness where, but for the grace of God, they would have been utterly destroyed. Remembrance of the Divine mercy is one of the great themes of the Book of Deuteronomy [eg 8.2, 18; 10.12-15; 15.15; 24.18, 22; 26.5-10].

*V*11: God had raised up prophets to guide them and specially dedicated men to act as the salt [*Matt* 5.13] of their society. But –

*V*12: They had attempted to pervert the Nazarites who were pledged to abstain from wine and (with menace and insolence) they had commanded the prophets to be silent.
  Remember that to insult the Lord's men is to insult the Lord Himself, for they are His ambassadors; hence the incidents recorded in 2 *Kings* 1 and 2 *Kings* 2.23-25.

## *V*13-16: THE JUDGEMENT TO COME

*V*13: **Behold I am pressed under you . . .** This may be read in two ways:

1. The Authorised Version, supported by the New American Standard Bible and the Revised Authorised, gives the sense that Jehovah is weighted down by the burden of His people's sin. Calvin prefers this sense and Matthew Henry gives it his first comment.
2. The RSV translates – 'I will press you down'. This sense is supported in a marginal comment in the Authorised Version, by the New International Version (1984), *Living Prophecies* and the Berkeley version. If this rendering is correct the words point to the fearsome judgement of God which will eventually be unleashed. This is the sense commented on by Poole and Lange and is accepted as a valid alternative by Matthew Henry.

Both interpretations are theologically correct. God *is* burdened with grief at the sinfulness of His people; thus Christ weeps over Jerusalem even as He pronounces judgement

[41]

upon it! Equally He makes clear that persistent sin cannot escape the weight of the consuming wrath of Divine Justice.

*V*14-16: All the human resources in which they have trusted will be found wanting [*cf Jer* 17.5].

The swift of foot will stumble and fall.

The strong will not be able to muster his forces.

The archers, though strong of arm, will be overwhelmed.

The swift runners will not be able to run fast enough to get away.

Cavalry horses will not be swift enough to carry their riders to safety.

Courageous men will throw away their weapons, discard clothing and run for their lives.


FOR MEDITATION

1. *V*6-8: To turn away from God opens the way to materialism, greed, self-indulgence, corruption and oppression. How easily men become avarious and twisted!

   (i) Authority becomes corrupt, and not only through bribes offered in cash! Our 'fair dealings' may be twisted by prejudice, personal or family relationships, or the anticipation of favours to be shown on our behalf.

   (ii) Heartless oppression may emerge from monopoly or even trade union domination, from educational as well as racial discrimination!

   (iii) Unscrupulous and careless greed is seen wherever men turn their back on human need, or exploit the emergency of war, disease and famine.

   (iv) Even religion can become twisted, elaborate in ritual yet careless of morality and empty of human kindness.

2. *V*9-10: How matchless is the grace that has redeemed us! Redemption by the blood of Christ! Victory over enemies! Continual guidance! [*Col* 2,6-7, 14-15]. We should diligently remind ourselves of the price paid. 'Thou shalt remember thou wast a bondman . . . and the Lord thy God redeemed thee' [*Deut* 15.15].

3. *V*11-12: God has given to us all the benefits of His revelation,

including the WORD of the Gospel in our own tongue, and the help of His Holy Spirit. What of our response? Have we listened as we should or turned a deaf ear to the preaching of the doctrines of grace. Or have we tried perversely to turn the 'separated' into worldly paths by sneering at their enthusiasm or pronouncing their sacrifice a waste of talent?

4. *V*13: How the Lord must be weighted down with our continual short-comings and indifference! Yet it is not too late for us to repent! Remember *Rom* 2.4-5. The consideration of how patient the Lord has been with us should excite our love and gratitude, and silence our natural tendency to complain at His disciplines. Whatever He has done with us is infinitely less in severity than we deserved. Remember also that the threat of judgement is as real as the promise of grace [*Matt* 23.37; *Luke* 13.3].

5. Spurgeon thus closed a sermon based on the phrase 'a cart full of sheaves': 'By time, by eternity, by life, by death, by heaven, by hell, I do conjure you believe in Him who is able to save unto the uttermost them that come unto Him. But if you believe not that Christ is He, you will die in your sins. After death the judgement! . . . After judgement, to a soul that is out of Christ, Hell! . . . Trust Jesus with your soul . . . Wilt thou? Nay, I know thou wilt not unless the Spirit of God shall constrain thee . . . God help you to come, God make you come, for Christ's sake!'

6. *V*14-16: Human strength of itself will never be sufficient to satisfy the demands of Divine judgement or fulfil the Lord's commission to service [2 *Cor* 3.5]. In the last analysis strength is a moral matter. A man like Paul can say, 'When I am weak, then am I strong' [2 *Cor* 12.10], because he had learned that true strength is from God [*Ps* 27.1, 46.1].

# 4: *The First Prophetic Discourse*

Chapter 3 *VI-15*

1 Hear this word that the Lord hath spoken against you, O children of Israel, against the whole family which I brought up from the land of Egypt, saying,

2 You only have I known of all the families of the earth: therefore I will punish you for all your iniquities.

3 Can two walk together, except they be agreed?

4 Will a lion roar in the forest, when he hath no prey? will a young lion cry out of his den, if he have taken nothing?

5 Can a bird fall in a snare upon the earth, where no gin is for him? shall one take up a snare from the earth, and have taken nothing at all?

6 Shall a trumpet be blown in the city, and the people not be afraid? Shall there be evil in a city, and the Lord hath not done it?

7 Surely the Lord God will do nothing, but he revealeth his secret unto his servants the prophets.

8 The lion hath roared, who will not fear? the Lord God hath spoken, who can but prophesy?

9 Publish in the palaces at Ashdod, and in the palaces in the land of Egypt, and say, Assemble yourselves upon the mountains of Samaria, and behold the great

tumults in the midst thereof, and the oppressed in the midst thereof.

10 For they know not to do right, saith the Lord, who store up violence and robbery in their palaces.

11 Therefore thus saith the Lord God; An adversary there shall be even round about the land; and he shall bring down thy strength from thee, and thy palaces shall be spoiled.

12 Thus saith the Lord; As the shepherd taketh out of the mouth of the lion two legs, or a piece of an ear; so shall the children of Israel be taken out that dwell in Samaria in the corner of a bed, and in Damascus in a couch.

13 Hear ye, and testify in the house of Jacob, saith the Lord God, the God of hosts,

14 That in the day that I shall visit the transgressions of Israel upon him I will also visit the altars of Bethel: and the horns of the altar shall be cut off, and fall to the ground.

15 And I will smite the winter house with the summer house; and the houses of ivory shall perish, and the great houses shall have an end, saith the Lord.

*V*1: Both parts of the nation are indicted here because they failed to live up to their privileged calling. Those in the South felt superior because they had the temple and the throne of David, but they were not walking in obedience to the Lord's word. Mere orthodoxy is not enough (see John 8.31-36).

In this pronouncement of judgement three things are to be noted as developed in the whole prophecy:

1. It is temporal rather than final judgements which are being dealt with here.

2. There is a call to repent [5.14] even though the judgement is so richly deserved.

3. God has a remnant [9.9]. Israel will be sifted among other nations as grain in a sieve, but not one 'kernel' (truly contrite person) will be lost.

*V2*: The special privilege of Israel as God's chosen people brings a very special responsibility.

**Known.** Used of the special relationship between husband and wife – a unique and exclusive relationship. Israel is unique among the nations as the 'special treasure' of Jehovah [*Ex* 19.5]. Along with the privilege goes the responsibility of the wife. This is fourfold:

1. Faithful love – 'forsaking all other, keep thou only unto him'.
2. Subjection – in the best sense of willing and devoted service.
3. Close companionship – only thus can love thrive and faithful service be rendered.
4. Bearing children – Israel was intended to be a nation bearing spiritual children for the glory of God. This is reflected in *Ex* 12.24-27; *Deut* 6.4-7; 32.46-47; *Is* 49.18-23, 54.1; *Joel* 2.28.

Judgement upon sin will inevitably follow wilful failure to meet the responsibility. There is nothing soft about the Divine love; it is a holy love which demands whole-hearted obedience.

*V3*: Emphasizes the truth that to walk in fellowship there must be agreement [*cf* 1 *John* 1.7]. When men turn rebelliously to their own way fellowship is broken [*Ps* 66.18]. The social sins of Israel, their idolatrous worship, their trust in false gods were all a token of REBELLION! Under the old covenant as under the new [*John* 14.15, 15.14], when men love God they keep His commandments and His commandments are not grievous [1 *John* 5.3].

*V*4: The prophet's warning is likened to a lion's roar – a sure sign that there is danger ahead! When the Lord speaks by His prophets this is no empty warning! He means it! [*Matt* 24.28].

*V*5: Calvin sees in this verse two principles:
1. That calamity does not come by chance: it is God who stretches out His nets of judgement.
2. The fowler does not plan to return home with his nets empty, neither does God make these threatenings in vain. His threats are not 'empty bugbears'. He will not remove the net until He has His prey; the judgement is inescapable! Two modern translations emphasize that the punishment is well deserved:

'A trap does not snap shut unless it has been stepped on: your punishment is well deserved' – *Living Prophecies*.

'Can a bird fall in a snare upon the earth where there is no trap for him? Does a trap spring up from the ground when nothing at all has sprung it? – *Amplified Old Testament*.

*V*6: The voice of the prophet is likened to a warning trumpet. When the Lord's watchman sounds the warning trumpet there is every cause for fear. The gentle correction has been ignored, the wrath of God has been stirred; there should be urgency in man's response just as the trumpet call is to immediate action.

**Evil** [*cf Is* 45.7] Here used in the sense of adversity and affliction, certainly not of moral evil. Thus, in English law, the killing of a person by lightning would be termed an 'act of God', even though we ourselves are not qualified to form a judgement as to the divine reason for the infliction of the 'evil'. Calvin comments thus on the last part of the verse:

'Unexpectedly indeed calamity comes, and it is commonly ascribed to chance. But the prophet here reminds us that God stretches His nets, in which men are caught, though they think that chance rules, and observe not the hand of God. They are deceived, he says: for the bird foresees not the ensnaring prepared for him; but yet he *falls* not *on the earth without the fowler*; for nets weave not themselves by chance, but they are made by the industry of the man who catches birds. So also calamities do not happen by chance, but proceed from the secret purposes of God'. Calvin adds a caution that we must not press the similitude too far, so as to lead any to think that God leads men to commit evil. The point is that He 'catches' men who do commit evil.

*V*7: The Lord does not act without giving warning and 'time to repent' [*Rev* 2.21]. He has chosen to reveal Himself, and this applies to judgement as well as salvation. In both cases this is an act of grace; He did not have to save, or reveal salvation. We must remember too that the penalty of sin is already written large on the pages of history. There is no reason why He should continue to warn us afresh that the wages of sin is death. That He does so is an abundant testimony to His grace.

The prophet here is viewed as standing in an intimate and responsible relationship to God. He is permitted to look into the secrets of Jehovah and from the privilege stems the responsibility to forewarn of judgement or offer salvation.

*V*8: The prophet cannot but speak. He is under the constraint of the Word of God [*Ezek* 2.5-7; 1 *Cor* 9.16; 2 *Pet* 1.20-21].

*V*9: The nations are called upon to hear the message of judgement and gather to see its fulfilment so that they might understand that the catastrophes coming upon Israel were due to sins which had stirred Israel's God to anger. Israel's adversaries were raised up by Him to forward His purposes.

*V*10: The disasters are directly related to particular sins of the nation. The wealthy homes (palaces) of the nobles and men of wealth were the repositories of luxury obtained through violence, selfishness and greed. It is worth noting that the sins especially indicated here are the social and economic ones [cf Is 1.16-17].

*V*11: The prophecy was fulfilled to the letter within fifty years by the Assyrians. Tiglath-Pileser III, Shalmaneser V and Sargon II were the monarchs who brought Samaria low. Amos never actually mentions Assyria in his prophecy (in the Septuagint translation, however, 'the Assyrians' take the place of 'Ashdod' in verse 9).

*V*12: Thus says the Lord, 'As the shepherd rescues out of the mouth of the lion two legs, or a piece of an ear, so shall the children of Israel who dwell in Samaria be rescued, with the corner of a couch and part of the damask covering of a bed'. – so *Amplified* OT (RSV omits 'the damask covering').

Here we have a picture of the devastation of Israel though there is perhaps a suggestion of a 'remnant' here. This is brought out in '*Living Prophecies*' – 'When the Israelites in Samaria are finally rescued, all they will have left is half a chair and a tattered pillow'.

Calvin suggests that the idea here is that those dwelling at ease in Samaria will soon have their illusion shattered and only a few will escape as by a miracle. There will be a complete overthrow of those who count themselves secure in wanton luxury and self-indulgence.

*V*13: The warning is now re-emphasized.

**House of Jacob** – not 'Israel' but 'Jacob' – the name of the deceiver and supplanter, perhaps intended to indicate a nation reverted to rebellion and sin. The name of God emphasizes His power as well as His covenant love. Because He is the covenant Lord, He will call His people to account [*Chap* 3.2]: because He is the Lord of hosts, He will be accomplishing His sovereign will even through the heathen nations soon to devastate Israel.

[49]

*V*14: Judgement is announced on the seat of false worship at Bethel. 1 *Kings* 13.1-6 is a historical foreshadowing of the judgement now to be exacted in full. Bethel is typical of a debased worship of God where the injunction of *Deut* 7.1-6 has not been observed [for NT enactment see 2 *Cor* 6.14].

*V*15: The days of ease and prosperity will be brought to a catastrophic end. The wealth implied here, and the destruction, have been fully confirmed by archaeological researches at the site of ancient Samaria where, for instance, fragments of the ivory ornamentations of great houses have been found. The fate of this city is a warning against concentration on material things. See *Matt* 6.29-34 and *Luke* 12.15; and compare the teaching of *Haggai* 1.6-7. The main sins denounced in these verses include:

1. Irresponsibility in the face of privilege.
2. Materialism and its accompanying self-indulgence and heartlessness.
3. False religion and idolatry.

FOR MEDITATION
1. Chapter 3.2. From this verse and its context we may deduce that:
    (i) agreement is the condition of walking together [*Ps* 40.8].
    (ii) sin is the obstacle to walking together [2 *Cor* 6.16].
    (iii) joy is the outcome of walking together [*Ps* 16.11].
2. Chapter 3.2. 'You only have I known'. Have I given myself to Him as completely as He has given Himself to me? [*Rom* 12.1-2]
    (i) Is my love exclusive? Is *Ps* 73.25 true of me?
    (ii) Am I prepared, like Paul, to be the willing bondslave of Jesus Christ 'whose service is perfect freedom'?
    (iii) Do I enjoy close companionship with the Lord through prayer, reading the Word, and other means of grace? Is my time with Him the most sacred and important part of the day?
    (iv) Am I bearing spiritual children? [*Prov* 11.30].
3. Chapter 3.3. Is there real agreement between the Lord and ourselves resulting in communion, communication, understanding, and on my part, obedience. [1 *John* 5.3]. He is abundantly willing to make

[50]

His abode with me. [*Rev* 3.20] Can I honestly say that by His grace the door of my heart opens to Him? Are my thoughts, ambitions, affections, time, home, money at his disposal? Let us ask ourselves these practical questions –

(i) Do I see myself as He sees me? [*Is* 64.6].

(ii) Do I really love His law and is it my meditation all the day? [*Ps* 119.97].

(iii) Does *Prov* 6.22 really represent my experience of His Word?

(iv) Does Jesus Christ have the pre-eminence in my life that He has in the purposes of God? [*Col* 1.18].

(v) Can I honestly say that *Phil* 3.8-14 represents my ambition?

(vi) Am I prepared to measure up to the responsibilities of knowing Him? [Check with *Luke* 6.45-46].

4. 'Can two walk together except they be agreed?' Hear a word from Spurgeon as he preached from this verse: 'We must be agreed with God as to the end of our Christian existence. God has formed us for Himself, that we may show forth His praise. The main end of a Christian man is that, having been bought with precious blood, he may live unto Christ, and not unto himself . . . I pray God that I may feel *that I am God's man*, that I have not a hair on my head which is not consecrated, nor a drop of blood which is not dedicated to His cause . . . I pray that selfishness may clean die out of you, that you may be able to say without any straining of the truth, "I have nothing to care for, nor to live for in this world but that I may glorify God and spread forth the savour of my Saviour's name." We cannot expect the Master's blessing till we are agreed about this.

Spurgeon also affords us a practical example of the outworking of this principle:

'A young couple, deeply in love, were considering marriage, when the lady discovered to her dismay that her fiancé not only had no interest in what constituted true religion, but had no regard for religion in general. After she had given him a gentle reproof he replied that a man of the world could not be so old-fashioned as to regard God and religion. Taking her courage into both hands the lady sadly but firmly replied, "From this moment, when I find that you have neither regard for God nor religion, I cease to be yours. A man who does not love and honour God can never love his wife constantly and sincerely. We shall have to part." '

[51]

5. Am I self-indulgent like the Jews against whom Amos prophesied, selfish and possessive in both spiritual and material things? It is easy for Christians to become happy and comfortable in the enjoyment of the fellowship and assurance afforded by the Christin life, and yet be without thought or concern for others. This involves the grieving of the Holy Spirit [*Eph* 4.30].

6. All Christians must and will appear before the judgement seat of Christ in the day of Christ [see *Rom* 14.10-12; 2 *Cor* 5.10; and compare with *Jer* 17.10].

7. Chapter 3.7 stresses the authority of the prophetic message [See 1 *Kings* 22. 13-14, and in the New Testament 2 *Tim* 3.15-16; 1 *Peter* 1.10-12; 2 *Peter* 1.20-21].

8. On *V*7 a paragraph from Spurgeon reminds us how this is at times experienced as the word is preached. 'How singularly at times you have heard your case described! You have gone to the house of God and sat down in the pew, and the minister has gone into the pulpit and taken a text just adapted to yourself. He begins to tell you what your position is exactly, and then he tells you the way you should go. You cannot help saying as you retire, "That man is a prophet". Aye, and so he is; for as you will remember, I have often told you this is the way to be a true servant of the Lord. Daniel was acknowledged to be a true servant of the Lord because he could tell the king both his dream and its interpretation. The astrologers could only tell the interpretation after they had been told the dream. Many can give you advice when they know your case; but the true servant of the Lord does not want to be informed about your case; he knows it beforehand. . . . This is the way to tell a true prophet of the Lord, and I beseech you believe no other.'

9. Chapter 3. 9-15 supplies an emphasis on the sovereignty of God that should never be forgotten by the believer. He is as much sovereign in the judgement of sin as in the salvation of sinners.

10. The awful character of the Divine judgement when it falls shows that it is lunacy to regard it lightly. Recall the solemn word of Jesus in *Matt* 10.28.

11. If this is the account God takes of sin in His own people, what will be the end of those who refuse to obey the Gospel of God? [1 *Peter* 4.17-18].

12. From *V*9 we may infer that when the nations are called to observe

the judgement upon Israel they are being warned of their own impending doom. Men also are to learn to view the chastening of others as a warning to themselves; a call to self-examination and humility.

13. In face of such solemn warnings the repentant believer needs the comfort of these eternal truths:

(i) The Lord our Father is the Sovereign who works all things according to the counsel of His own will [*Eph* 1.11].

(ii) He chose us as 'sons of Jacob', perverse men; He was fully aware of the iniquity of our hearts. Though He may need to cripple us [*Gen* 32.25] He will surely make us children of Israel (a prince with God). [See *Phil* 1.6].

(iii) All things work together for good to those who love God, who are the called according to His purpose [*Rom* 8.28].

Chapter 4 *V*1-13

1 Hear this word, ye kine of Bashan, that are in the mountain of Samaria, which oppress the poor, which crush the needy, which say to their masters, Bring, and let us drink.

2 The Lord God hath sworn by his holiness, that, lo, the days shall come upon you, that he will take you away with hooks, and your posterity with fish-hooks.

3 And ye shall go out at the breaches, every cow at that which is before her; and ye shall cast them into the palace, saith the Lord.

4 Come to Bethel, and transgress; at Gilgal multiply transgression; and bring your sacrifices every morning and your tithes after three years.

5 And offer a sacrifice of thanksgiving with leaven, and proclaim and publish the free offerings; for this liketh you, O ye children of Israel, saith the Lord God.

6 And I also have given you cleanness of teeth in all your cities, and want of bread in all your places: yet have ye not returned unto me, saith the Lord.

7 And also I have withholden the rain from you, when there were yet three months to the harvest: and I caused it to rain upon one city, and caused

it not to rain upon another city: one piece was rained upon, and the piece whereupon it rained not withered.

8 So two or three cities wandered unto one city, to drink water; but they were not satisfied: yet have ye not returned unto me, saith the Lord.

9 I have smitten you with blasting and mildew: when your gardens and your vineyards and your fig trees and your olive trees increased, the palmerworm devoured them: yet have ye not returned unto me, saith the Lord.

10 I have sent among you the pestilence after the manner of Egypt: your young men have I slain with the sword, and have taken away your horses; and I have made the stink of your camps to come up unto your nostrils: yet have ye not returned unto me, saith the Lord.

11 I have overthrown some of you, as God overthrew Sodom and Gomorrah, and ye were as a firebrand plucked out of the burning: yet have ye not returned unto me, saith the Lord.

12 Therefore thus will I do unto thee, O Israel: and because I will do this unto thee, prepare to meet thy God, O Israel.

13 For, lo, he that formeth the mountains, and createth the wind, and declareth unto man what is his thought, that maketh the morning darkness, and treadeth upon the high places of the earth, The Lord, The God of hosts, is his name.'

*V*1-3: THE FATE OF THE WEALTHY WOMEN OF SAMARIA

*V*1: **Kine** – cows. This is not a very polite way to address a dowager duchess but it does give a very fair estimate of these women, immersed as they were in the indulgence of their animal appetites.

**Bashan** was an area, east of Jordan, where the pasture was very lush and verdant.

**Which oppress the poor** – They encouraged their husbands' oppressions because they were continually making expensive demands. We are reminded that we are responsible not only for what we do but also for what we inspire others to do.

**Bring and let us drink.** In ancient society, as in modern, social evils were aggravated by the love of strong drink. The Book of Proverbs is rich in warnings. *eg* 20.1; 23.20-21, 29-32; 31.4-5.

*V*2: **The Lord God hath sworn by his holiness.** The holiness of God is one of the great themes of this prophecy; it suggests His personal presence and transcendent 'otherness'! His perfect moral nature makes clear His demands upon those who are His people. His people were intended to be different, and this spot-lights their failure; they had not maintained their separation but had fallen into the sins of the surrounding nations, especially idolatry, oppression and the various forms of self-indulgence.

Calvin would translate 'by His sanctuary' instead of 'by His holiness', thus contrasting the Divinely appointed sanctuary with the multitudes of false sanctuaries. Many modern scholars allege that Amos would not be interested in the 'Cultic Symbol', but that is pure conjecture: after all, he was a Southerner. Whilst worship must not be allowed to fall to the level of mere routine and ritual performance, there is a place for due order in religion. Remember *John* 4.23-24; also read 2 *Sam* 6.

The last part of the verse foretells captivity and servitude. The evil-doers will be dragged from their houses as fish are drawn from the sea by hooks. Compare with this the imagery of *Jer* 16.16.

*V*3: The general idea is that of the ignominy of captivity.

These elegant women will be led out like a herd of cows. The last part of the verse is not easy to translate but the sense is obvious enough. Calvin renders it, 'Ye shall throw yourselves down from the palace'.

*Living Prophecies* renders: (the whole verse) 'You will be hauled from your beautiful homes and tossed out through the nearest breach in the wall'. The idea is of panic or captivity or both! Ease, luxury, security, will all be shattered. God's Word continually warns against becoming immersed in the things of this world and points us to their essential insecurity. [*James* 4.13-14].

### V4-5: HERE WE HAVE IRONIC INDICTMENT OF EMPTY RELIGION

*V4*: **Bethel** and **Gilgal** were two of the main centres of worship in Israel. Both had sacred associations with the worship of Jehovah as we see from *Gen* 28.16-22 and *Josh* 5.9, but they had now become centres of 'syncretism' – the worship of Jehovah was conducted with all manner of device and ceremony culled from the heathen nations round about. There was much ritual and empty show but a complete lack of true sincerity which would be evidenced by heartfelt repentance. Instead there was religious prostitution and the sanction of every kind of vice and immorality in flagrant breach of God's commandments.

**Tithes after three years** – RV and RSV 'Tithes every three days.' The ritual was being carried on with exaggerated scrupulosity but had no meaning for God.

*V5*: **A sacrifice of thanksgiving with leaven** – See *Exod* 23.18; *Lev* 2.11, 7.13, 23.17.

The loaves offered at the feast of weeks and the sacrifices of thanksgiving mentioned in *Lev* 7.13 were the only ones allowed with leaven, which was regarded as the symbol of corruption. When authorized for use, the leaven was rendered inoperative by the fire of the altar. There is here probably a double idea:

1. Great pretence of thankfulness and much religious show. Sacrifices of thanksgiving were commonly offered after deliverances from special danger or physical sickness.
2. This style of offering is pleasing to the natural appetite; leavened bread is more attractive to the taste. Here is a religion pleasing to the natural man, full of show and pretended gratitude but lacking the essential elements of self-denial and true repentance [cf Ps 51.17; Jer 5.31; Mic 6.6-8].

### V6-13: THESE VERSES SHOW HOW GOD APPLIED THE ROD OF CHASTENING IN VARIOUS WAYS BUT HAD BEEN MET BY STUBBORN IMPENITENCE

V6: Famine had first of all been used to chasten them but they had not responded to the correction by returning to God.

V7: The second method of chastening was by drought. In the providence of God this had not been inflicted on all parts of the land. The rod of correction had been employed with mercy.

V8: They had suffered inconvenience but not complete disaster. However, as with the famine, this had not turned them back to the Lord.

V9: Further pestilences of various kinds had been employed – blight, mildew, locust.

The damage thus far had been without loss of human life. Even in wrath the Lord had remembered mercy.

V10: The judgements spoken of here were much more severe, involving, first of all, plague and secondly, slaughter in battle. Egypt was notorious as a land which was prone to plagues. The reference may be to the plagues upon Egypt in Moses' day.

V11: The disaster spoken of here may well be the earthquake

of Chapter 1.1. Even in the midst of such a judgement there was a suggestion of mercy. They were as a firebrand plucked from the burning. The overthrow had not been so utter and complete as in the case of Sodom and Gomorrah. This was not because they were less wicked but because God in sovereign grace chose to temper judgement with mercy. Here was discipline, not destruction! (see also *Zech* 3.2).

It is worth noting that the progressive severity of the judgements follows the pattern prophesied in *Deut* 28.

*V*12: In view of their continued non-repentance and obduracy in sin, God will bring further judgements upon them. Since they will not meet with Him and walk with Him in grace, they will meet with Him in judgement.

*V*13: The truth and reality in the background of these thoughts are found in the nature of God Himself.

  (i) He is the Creator.

  (ii) He is omniscient, the One who knows all things. He can read and foretell the thoughts of man.

  (iii) He is omnipotent, transforming light into darkness, the God of the impossible [*Gen* 18.14].

  (iv) He is the God of terrible majesty, treading upon the high places of the earth.

  (v) He is the God of hosts, the commander of the forces of Heaven. There is no limit to His resources or His power.

Yet for all these attributes He is the God of this small people, the God who can be met through grace.

Notice that though Amos was one of the earliest of the prophets there is nothing crude or underdeveloped in his knowledge and conception of God.

FOR MEDITATION

1. Am I so self-centred in my personal and spiritual life that I may justly be numbered with the 'fat cows'? The Christian can be a parasite by continually demanding attention, and by taking all the

fellowship the Church has to offer without accepting the responsibilities involved. Am I asset or liability to my fellow-Christians?

2. I am to remember that I am guilty not only of the sins I commit but also of those I inspire. God will hold me responsible for my impact on others. I can lead men into wrong, pressure them into it, inspire them or oppress them!

3. What of my worship? it may be scrupulous and full of ritual, yet completely worthless in the sight of God. I may be sound in doctrine and full of intellectual knowledge of Scripture, yet barren of grace. Even my giving, though extensive, may be futile! Contrast *Matt* 6.2. and *Luke* 21.1-4.

4. Is there a Bethel or a Gilgal in my life which has become obnoxious to God?

   (i) A place of meeting with God and covenanting with Him which has now become empty of reality? I may hold on to the language of salvation and devotion when it no longer has any valid content in my life.

   (ii) A place of repentance where reproach was put away? I may continue to subscribe to 'the form of sound words' when all manner of worldly thinking has entered into my life.

5. [V6-10] Are there things happening to me now which the Lord intends me to see as His disciplines to call me back to Himself? Famine, drought, pestilence, defeat may be spiritual experiences. Is the Lord allowing these as warnings that I am drifting away from Him?

6. (i) 'A firebrand plucked from the burning'. Not all Christians have a vivid testimony or a past full of murk and mischief in the eyes of the world, but I need to recall that all are brands plucked from the burning [see *Eph* 2.1]. Am I as grateful as I should be? Do I serve as wholeheartedly as I should? [*Rom* 12.1-2]. Do I remember, when dealing with straying folk, 'There, but for the grace of God, go I?' [see *Gal* 6.1].

   (ii) The phrase causes me to face: *a.* The universality of sin, *b.* My understanding of salvation, *c.* The unsearchableness of God's love.

   (iii) I have been purchased at infinite cost – The PRICE of salvation. It appeared impossible that it could happen – The POWER of salvation. I have been effectively rescued from eternal loss – The PERFECTION of salvation.

7. A very vivid illustration of what it is to be a 'brand plucked from the burning' is seen in the testimony of Thomas Olivers, author of the hymn 'The God of Abraham praise' – On account of his use of oaths and evil language, he says 'I was generally reckoned the worst boy who had been in these parts (Montgomeryshire) for the last twenty or thirty years . . . I went one Sabbath Day to St Chad's Church (Shrewsbury) in company with a very wicked young man. We got into the organ loft, and while the late Dr Adams was preaching, I was wantonly cursing him and almost every sentence which proceeded out of his mouth . . . Not long after, a young man and I, after committing a most notorious and shameful act of arch-villainy, of which I was the contriver, agreed to leave the country together . . . he, leaving his apprenticeship, and I several debts behind us, which was generally my case wherever I went . . . After some days we got to Bristol . . . One night I met a multitude of people and asked one of them where they had been. She answered, "To hear Mr Whitefield". She also told me he was to preach the next night. I went, but was too late. The following evening I was determined to be in time: accordingly I went near three hours before the time. When the service began I did little but look about me, but on seeing the tears trickle down the cheeks of some who stood near me, I became more attentive.

'The text was, "Is not this a brand plucked out of the fire?" When this sermon began I was certainly a dreadful enemy to God and to all that is good, and one of the most profligate and abandoned young men living; but by the time it was ended I was become a new creature. For, in the first place, I was deeply convinced of the great goodness of God towards me all my life, particularly in that He had given His Son to die for me. I had also a far clearer view of all my sins, particularly my base ingratitude towards Him. These discoveries quite broke my heart, and caused showers of tears to trickle down my cheeks. I was likewise filled with an utter abhorrence of my evil ways, and was much ashamed that I had ever walked in them . . . I broke off all my evil practices, and forsook all my wicked and foolish companions without delay, and gave myself up to God and His service with my whole heart. O, what reason have I to say, "Is not this a brand plucked out of the fire?"

'When I returned to my lodgings the people saw that something remarkable had befallen me, and as they knew not where I had been, could not imagine what it was. They were greatly astonished the following days on seeing me weep almost incessantly . . . When they put it to me, I frankly told them the whole matter; and though the best of them was but half-hearted in religion, yet they all rejoiced at the mighty change they saw in me!'

8. 'Prepare to meet thy God!' Here is the inescapable assize. How shall I stand? [*Matt* 25.31–33].

(i) God is interested in men.

(ii) Men need preparation to meet God – He is in fact the only source of all that men need – revelation, repentance, redemption.

(iii) There is a meeting which men cannot escape [*Acts* 17.31].

9. Consider Him – THY GOD [*Ps* 50.7].

(i) He made you – CREATION [*Gen* 1.26-27].

(ii) He cares for you – PROVIDENCE[*James* 1.17].

(iii) He alone can deliver you from sin – SALVATION [*Is* 45.22].

(iv) Present yourself to Him [*Rom* 12.2].

10. A famous preacher named Madan, educated for the bar, owed his conversion to the Christian faith to the following circumstances. One evening his boon companions, gathered in a coffee house, urged him to go to hear John Wesley preach at a place not far away, in order to mimic his mannerisms and mode of speech before them on his return. This was to be their evening's entertainment. At the moment when Madan entered the preaching place Wesley read as his text, 'Prepare to meet thy God'. The solemn accent excited his immediate attention and his seriousness increased as the sermon proceeded and included an exhortation to repentance. When Madan returned to the coffee-house his companions asked if he could take off the old Methodist. 'No, gentlemen', he replied, 'but he has taken me off'. From that time he forsook their company, met with true Christians, and became both a godly man and a powerful preacher.

# 6: *The Third Prophetic Discourse*

## SUMMARY OF MESSAGE

The section opens with an announcement of the terrible doom which awaits the nation and is at its very doors [5.2-3]. This threat is employed as the ground for an earnest call to repent even at this late hour [5.4-15]. The Day of the Lord will be a day of utter darkness because their religion, practised in the Name of God, is not at all in accordance with His will and with the standards He has expressed [5.16-27]. The section proceeds to supply further details of the disaster soon to befall this rebellious people [6.1-14].

Chapter 5 *V*1-3

1 **Hear ye this word which I take up against you, even a lamentation, O house of Israel.**

2 **The virgin of Israel is fallen; she shall no more rise: she is forsaken upon her land; there is none to raise her up.**

3 **For thus saith the Lord God; The city that went out by a thousand shall leave an hundred, and that which went forth by an hundred shall leave ten, to the house of Israel.**

*V*1: **A lamentation.** There is always a note of sorrow linked with Divine judgement. We have a vivid illustration of this in the weeping of Christ over Jerusalem and its approaching

desolation [*Luke* 19.41-44]. From this we may take the following lessons:

1. Sin must ultimately bring sorrow and ruin [*Is* 17.11; *Rom*
6.23: *Gal* 6.8]. In the last analysis our sin will find us out.
[*Num* 32.23].

2. The judgement of God upon sin is never heartless. It is to
be viewed against the background of His love and compassion. The God who dealt with sin at Calvary can never
be accused of lack of understanding.

3. Sin causes grief to the heart of God [*Gen* 6.6]. He did not
create man to sin and to suffer in this way but 'to glorify
God and to enjoy Him for ever!' [Shorter Catechism]

4. Though God loves so greatly, He will not 'spoil' us. He
loves with a holy love which cannot tolerate sin. As sons
and daughters we need chastening [*Heb* 12.6] and such
correction is an evidence of love, indicating that we are
truly His children.

*V*2: **Virgin.** Some suggest:

1. That in the prophets the term 'virgin' is sometimes used to
symbolize a nation living in self-indulgence and luxury
[*Is* 47.1]. Calvin favours this interpretation here (this is the
first occasion in Scripture where the word 'virgin' is used
in this fashion).

2. That the expression is symbolic of the fact that Israel as a
kingdom had not previously been subdued by a foreign
power.

3. That the expression speaks of Israel's pristine purity, beauty
and separation to God.

Two further ideas may be emphasized:

(i) The Lord looks upon Israel with the tender protective-
ness of a father for his daughter or of the husband for his
young bride.

(ii) The Lord also puts forward the rightful claim of the
husband that his bride should belong to him alone. This

is the meaning of the expression 'The Lord thy God is a jealous God'.

This is the way in which Christ regards His Church [2 Cor 11.2]. He sees us not as we are by nature, filthy in our sin, but as grace re-makes us – pure, separated to Himself.

This is why turning away from God is such a tragedy: it is turning from the highest and purest and best. The way of sin is inevitably downward. We need to remember that when the way seems very hard [Prov 23.17-18] ease and destruction often go together [Matt 7.13-14]. The right way will be tough. It is not easy to remain a 'virgin' when faced with the clamouring demands of the flesh, but this is the only way of entering into the fullness of joy in communion with the Beloved [Jas 4.4]. Our purity must come from Christ. The virgin in the ancient world was so because she was under protection – that was why she wore a veil – she was in subjection to her father or her husband; they were her protection! So it is with the believer and Christ.

**She is forsaken.** The friendship of her pretended allies fails in time of trouble. This lesson is vividly taught in the prophecy of Hosea [2.7] where Gomer, the prophet's unfaithful wife, is a type of Israel. The story of the Prodigal Son in the New Testament teaches a similar truth [Luke 15.13-16]. There are two lessons implied here:

a. The friendship of the world fails in time of trouble.

b. Not only is the world inconstant, it is incapable of helping in the desperate plight into which sin brings us.

V3: The awfulness of Israel's plight is pictured here in terms of a ninety per cent slaughter.

FOR MEDITATION
1. A Lamentation. If we saw sin as God sees it, and realized the awfulness of its consequences we could not be so indifferent to the fate

of those who are without Christ or so slack in our stewardship of the truth.

2. The Virgin. As Christians we have been betrothed to Christ as a pure virgin.

(i) The symbol of purity, beauty, and separation [*Eph* 5.25-27].

(ii) The symbol of inviolacy. Because of Christ's protection the virgin is not overwhelmed by enemies. Think of the assurance as well as the responsibilities expressed in 1 *Cor* 6.19-20. If we are the temple of the Holy Spirit, our bodies, minds and souls are to be kept for Christ alone. At the same time, since He is the Spirit of power, He is able to keep us in peace and purity [*Rom* 8.11].

(iii) The veil of subjection. The wife must own the fact by wearing her veil. Our spiritual veil is one of obedience to Christ. This is the supreme evidence that we are truly His.

(iv) The virgin 'falls' when she casts off her subjection: she then becomes prey to every prowling wolf and ravaging lion.

(v) Isaac Watts, in the magnificent hymn 'Join all the glorious names', closes with a fine sense of Christian assurance when he writes:

> *Should all the hosts of death,*
> *And powers of hell unknown,*
> *Put their most dreadful forms*
> *Of rage and mischief on,*
> *I shall be safe, for Christ displays*
> *Superior power and guardian grace'.*

3. William Cowper expresses the dedication of the Christian well when he writes:

> *Lord, I would indeed submit,*
> *Gladly yield my all to Thee:*
> *What Thy wisdom sees most fit*
> *Must be surely best for me.*
> *Only when the way is rough,*
> *And the coward flesh would start,*[1]
> *Let Thy promise and Thy love*
> *Cheer and animate my heart.*

[1] shrink back

4. Forsaken.

   (i) The despair of men apart from God's help. The most heartfelt
     agony that man can know is that of feeling FORSAKEN [Ps 22.1;
     Lam 1.1-4, 3.1-18].

   (ii) The disillusionment of men with their false 'loves' – they fail
     [Jer 2.13], they forsake [Jer 30.14].

   (iii) The determination of the heavenly love [Is 49.14-16, 62.4;
     Jer 31.3].

Chapter 5 V4-15

4 For thus saith the Lord unto the house of Israel, Seek
ye me, and ye shall live:

5 But seek not Bethel, nor enter into Gilgal, and pass
not to Beer-sheba: for Gilgal shall surely go into
captivity, and Bethel shall come to nought.

6 Seek the Lord, and ye shall live; lest he break out
like fire in the house of Joseph, and devour it, and
there be none to quench it in Bethel.

7 Ye who turn judgement to wormwood, and leave
off righteousness in the earth,

8 Seek him that maketh the seven stars and Orion, and
turneth the shadow of death into the morning, and
maketh the day dark with night; that calleth for the
waters of the sea, and poureth them out upon the face
of the earth: The Lord is his name:

9 That strengtheneth the spoiled against the strong, so
that the spoiled shall come against the fortress.

10 They hate him that rebuketh in the gate, and they
abhor him that speaketh uprightly.

11 Forasmuch therefore as your treading is upon the
poor, and ye take from him burdens of wheat: ye
have built houses of hewn stone, but ye shall not
dwell in them: ye have planted pleasant vineyards,
but ye shall not drink wine of them.

12 For I know your manifold transgressions and your
mighty sins: they afflict the just, they take a bribe, and

they turn aside the poor in the gate from their right.

13 Therefore the prudent shall keep silence in that time; for it is an evil time.

14 Seek good, and not evil, that ye may live: and so the Lord, the God of hosts, shall be with you, as ye have spoken.

15 Hate the evil, and love the good, and establish judgement in the gate: it may be that the Lord God of hosts will be gracious unto the remnant of Joseph.

*V*4: A call to repentance. The essence of repentance is not in things done but in an attitude to a person – **Seek ye me**! God demands earnestness in relation to His person [2 *Chron* 7.14]. All our actions in relation to repentance are to be an evidence of our desire to find Him and know Him. When thus He calls, us He lends us also the aid of His enabling Spirit, and He promises success [*Jer* 29.13]; we shall not search in vain, and when we find Him we find life. The teaching of the Old Testament is brought to full fruition in the New Testament [*John* 1.4, 17.3]. Earnestness alone is not enough: it must be linked with 'unity of heart' to be true obedience [1 *Sam* 15.22 2 *Kings* 10.15; *Amos* 3.3].

*V*5: A solemn warning that salvation will not be found through corrupt sanctuaries which God disowns. Bethel and Gilgal have already been mentioned [4.4] and now Beersheba is linked with them. Beersheba was one of the ancient sanctuaries of Judah on the Southern frontier towards Edom. It had hallowed associations [*Gen* 21.31] but had now become a centre of idolatry, even for Israelites from the Northern Kingdom [*Amos* 8.14].

1. Notice how the devil loves to penetrate the sacred in order to profane and pervert it. The very memorials of grace may be turned to abomination as in the Roman Catholic doctrine of the Mass.

2. There is a solemn warning against seeking salvation in institutions, formulae, or traditions, however venerable. We have an example of this danger in the superstitious attitude of Israel to the ark [1 *Sam* 4] and another in the veneration of the brazen serpent [2 *Kings* 18.4]. There is a deliberate contrast between *V*4 and 5 – the Person of God in *V*4 and the institution in *V*5.

3. Also implied is a condemnation of syncretism, allowing heathenish and unbiblical practices to influence our faith [see *Is* 52.11; 2 *Cor* 6.14-18]. We are to 'come out' because God brings us out [*Deut* 6.23]. Separation from the world is an essential aspect of our salvation [*James* 4.4; 1 *John* 2.15-17]. The last part of the verse is a play on words – 'Gilgal (The place of rolling) shall be rolled away, and Bethel (the House of God) shall become Beth-aven (the house of vanity).'

*V*6: The call to seek God is now repeated: to find Him is to find eternal life; but the ungodly nation is reminded of His holiness. There can be no communion between a Holy God and such an unclean people. The burning purity of His holiness will consume them. The sense of His holiness is well caught in Thomas Binney's hymn 'Eternal light, eternal light', especially in the lines

> *The spirits that surround Thy throne*
> *May bear the burning bliss.*

[see *Is* 33.14; 2 *Thess* 1.8-9; *Heb* 12.29].

*V*7: The consequences of their religious sins are now revealed in the social and moral sphere. These men of false religion had false social values too. They perverted justice and turned to uncontrolled self-will. 'Justice was turned into a bitter pill: righteousness and fair play became meaningless fictions'.

*V*8: Here we see Amos thinking of God as the Creator and Upholder of the whole universe. The herdman who often sat under the stars would appreciate the lessons they taught. The

Israelites were making of God a petty-minded deity who would be delighted by frivolous trifles. He was not to be worshipped as the heathen worshipped imaginary star deities. He made the stars! In place of such 'vain imaginations' proceeding from darkened hearts, Amos turns the evil-doers to the thought of the greatness and majesty of Jehovah, the God whom they despised and forsook. He declares Him to be the Lord of heaven above and of the earth beneath, creation's supreme Lord [cf Rev 4.11 and 5.13]. Three times in his prophecy Amos pronounces something akin to the Doxology, each time ending with the words, 'The Lord is His Name' [4.13, 5.8, 9.6], and in each case the words of praise are based upon the majesty of God as seen in the works of His hands. Isaac Watts echoes the thought in the words,

> I sing the almighty power of God
> That made the mountains rise,
> That spread the flowing seas abroad
> And built the lofty skies.

V9: The Lord employs His power not only in the physical but also in the moral realm. He 'shows himself strong' on behalf of the weak and down-trodden [2 Chron 16.9, Luke 1.51-53], strengthening the weakest to overthrow the strongest human defences. Human defences cannot withstand God's power. The greatest forces in the world are spiritual [Ps 127.1-2]. The *Amplified Old Testament* expresses this verse vividly – 'Who causes sudden destruction to flash forth upon the strong so that destruction comes upon the fortress'. The heathen thought of the stars as directing the course of history but it is He who made the stars who does so, and the ultimate evidence of His power is seen in His vindication of His own as 'poor and weak' – 'The lame take the prey.' [Is 33.23; cf 40.29].

V10: Here there is a further indictment of those labelled 'the strong' in the previous verse. Their strength has led them into arrogance and self-will. Not only are they not righteous, they hate all that stands for righteousness, since consistent righteousness is a constant rebuke to the ungodly. Feeling that they are being 'got at' they become bitter, resentful, and rebellious, as did those who stoned Stephen [*Acts* 7.54-60].

**Him that reproveth in the gate.** The gate was the place of meeting of the elders (rulers) of a city, so the phrase here may mean the counsellor or judge who dared to raise his voice in righteous reproof.

**They abhor him that speaketh uprightly**. They do not like straight speaking. Their lives are full of flattery and deceit.

*V*11-12 : Amos pronounces God's reaction to social unrighteousness. He particularly denounces the corruption of the judges. What hope is there for a nation when those who are responsible for setting moral standards have 'gone to seed'? Leadership in moral affairs involves a man in dreadful responsibilities, and Israel's leaders had wilfully turned aside to covetousness and violence.

*V*11 : **Treading upon the poor.** Oppression. This is not to be confined to violence but includes the grasping attitude which is careless of the other man's need [see 2 *Sam* 12.1-6].
**Houses of hewn stone: Vineyards.** Symbols of their false sense of security and desire for luxury.

In the same way the people of a later age were warned by Haggai that their concentration on material things to the neglect of the spiritual, would bring them no lasting blessing [*Hag* 1.6-7; *cf Ps* 127.1-2].

*V*12 : The Lord has taken note of their sin. It is worth observing that the oppression of the poor gives particular offence to God. So in the New Testament the only man who is deliberately spoken of as being in hell is the rich man who neglected to observe and assist the poor man in his need [*Luke* 16.19-31]. Compare the 'goats' in *Matt* 25.4-46.

*V*13: Since God is aware of these things the righteous need not perplex themselves [1 *Peter* 4.19]. There is no place for bitterness or resentment either in relation to God or to men. Neither take judgement into your own hands nor doubt the certainty or equity of the judgement of God. This is hard counsel to obey, but remember that David would not lay hands on Saul though now and again given ample opportunity [1 *Sam.* Chapters 24 and 26]. Calvin suggests that evil would be so prevalent that the protest of the prudent man would be quite unheeded.

*V*14-15: The call to repentance in verse 4 is now repeated in much more detail. The practical and ethical nature of repentance is strongly emphasized. There is to be an earnest longing for good and rejection of evil in the heart, matched by practical godly living.

*V*14: Compare 3.3 Can two walk together except they be agreed? Consider the case of Enoch whose pleasing of God was the outcome of faith and the obedience of faith [*Heb* 11.5-6].

*V*15: **It may be**. We are reminded that forgiveness is always a privilege and not a right. The fact that it is so freely offered should not cause us to presume upon it. Men are commanded to repent – this is their duty as moral creatures – but even where they do, this forgiveness is still an act of grace. Men are forgiven when they repent, not because they repent. The penalty of sin still hangs round the neck of the repentant one but for the grace of God, and the removal of sin by an accepted sacrifice.

**Remnant.** The idea of the 'saved remnant' is common prophetic teaching. It is particularly prominent in Isaiah and Jeremiah, but it is found also in several of the minor prophets. For its New Testament occurrences, see *Rom* 9.27 and 11.5.

**Of Joseph**. Joseph is mentioned in this verse (and in *V*6) because Ephraim, the leading tribe in the kingdom of Israel, traced its descent from Joseph [*Gen* 41.52].

1. *V*4-5: SEEK ME . . . SEEK NOT. We see here the proneness of the human heart to seek salvation in wrong ways. Remember *Prov.* 14.12, 16.25, *Jer* 10.23. Hence we have the multiplication of heresies, sects and cults. Empty observance of right forms of worship also is a real danger.

2. In *V*4 we are reminded that we are called to have personal dealings with the Lord Himself. The Christian disciple is not merely one who accepts a certain doctrine, he follows a Divine person [*Matt* 16.24-25; *Mark* 10.21].

3. From *V*5 observe that institutions, however venerable, may become corrupt. Our one safe refuge is in the Word God has given – this must be our rule of faith and practice. The best institutions can go bad or dead! Bethel, Gilgal, Beersheba were all places linked with Divine revelation, but we cannot rest in venerated human names or past tradition. Our only safe rest is the living God. The Church at Sardis [*Rev* 3.1] had a name that it lived but was dead.

4. From *V*8. The Lord who created is the Lord who redeems and re-creates.

5. In *V*7, 9-12, we see the Divine hatred of oppression. The Christian must not only not engage in evil practices, he must be prepared to speak out against them. Carelessness of the needs of others can cause oppression and poverty for which we share responsibility because of our lack of concern.

6. *V*12-15. Let the impenitent tremble.
   Let the righteous be still.
   Let those who are moved by fear repent and be saved.

   The Bible in a wonderful way balances the judgement and the grace of God. The fear of the Lord does not reduce a man to cowed servitude, it introduces him to willing and devoted obedience.

7. The believer is prudent: he has learned patience. He knows that the Lord will act in His own good time. He does not react in passion but walks by faith. [see *Ps* 37, especially *V*1-11].

8. *V*14-15.
   (i) A change of attitude – searching for good.
   (ii) A change of behaviour – resulting from a renewed heart.
   (iii) A change in relationship – the Lord with us.

(iv) A change in experience – the outcome of grace. Repentance involves a transformation of attitude, action and approach to life!

9. Since the Lord is the Creator of all, the One who controls history and determines the destiny of men, it is He who ultimately takes account of the behaviour of all men. The righteous can be at peace even in the evil days, knowing that He will vindicate His own holy Name and all those upon whom He bestows His love. In their own poor way they love Him in return. They are not to grow weary in well-doing, even in discouraging days: remember *Gal* 6.9.

Chapter 5 *V*16-27

**16** **Therefore the Lord, the God of hosts, the Lord, saith thus; Wailing shall be in all streets; and they shall say in all the highways, Alas! Alas! and they shall call the husbandman to mourning, and such as are skilful of lamentation to wailing.**

**17** **And in all vineyards shall be wailing: for I will pass through thee, saith the Lord.**

**18** **Woe unto you that desire the day of the Lord! to what end is it for you? the day of the Lord is darkness, and not light.**

**19** **As if a man did flee from a lion, and a bear met him; or went into the house, and leaned his hand on the wall, and a serpent bit him.**

**20** **Shall not the day of the Lord be darkness, and not light? even very dark, and no brightness in it?**

**21** **I hate, I despise your feast days, and I will not smell in your solemn assemblies.**

**22** **Though ye offer me burnt offerings and your meat offerings, I will not accept them; neither will I regard the peace offerings of your fat beasts.**

**23** **Take thou away from me the noise of thy songs; for I will not hear the melody of thy viols.**

**24** **But let judgement run down as waters, and righteousness as a mighty stream.**

25 Have ye offered unto me sacrifices and offerings in the wilderness forty years, O house of Israel?

26 But ye have borne the tabernacle of your Moloch and Chiun your images, the star of your god, which ye made to yourselves.

27 Therefore will I cause you to go into captivity beyond Damascus, saith the Lord, whose name is The God of hosts.

The thought now progresses to a more vivid presentation of the judgement to come: the false confidence of Israel in the Day of the Lord will be utterly shattered because their religion has been a foul thing in the sight of God.

*V*16: Deep anguish awaits Israel. Jamieson, Fausset and Brown's commentary suggests that when the husbandmen are called to mourning there is an insufficiency of paid mourners! Perhaps a more acceptable explanation is that the husbandmen are called to mourn because the national calamities are so extensive, The circumstances indicate an extreme situation. Remember that at the time when Amos prophesied the future seemed secure enough for Israel. They appeared to be 'getting away with it', but do not forget *Eccles* 8.11 and *Num* 32.23. The Christian needs to be reminded that though the Lord redeems from the destruction which would be our fate but for grace, we, no more than Israel of old, can afford to be presumptuous.

*V*17: **The vineyards** here symbolize the fruitfulness and joy of the nation. Even these will be reduced to mourning.

*V*18: Israel still had a nominal faith in God, and in their superficiality they thought that in the great Day of the Lord all would be well with them simply because they were the children of Abraham, Isaac and Jacob. There were those who were resting in the same false confidence in the days of John the Baptist, and who had to be reminded that God was able of the stones to raise up children to Abraham. Confidence in the flesh would be of no avail. Jesus also warned, in the parable of the ten virgins, of the foolishness of those who were eagerly expecting the Bridegroom's coming, (a similar idea to the day of the Lord), but had made no adequate preparation for it. They were expecting a day of glory but instead it would come as a day of judgement and sorrow. In similar fashion many religious people are resting nowadays in some fancied security of birth, ritual performance or credal profession.

*V*19: The prophet pictures vividly the awfulness of the day of the Lord. It will be as though a man fled from a lion only to be met by a bear, or as if he entered a house and rested against a wall, thinking himself secure, only to be bitten by a serpent.

We have various aspects of the judgement pictured here:
1. Its fierceness.
2. Its inescapability.
3. Its terror.

*V*20: Darkness is here used as the symbol of terror and doom. There will be no shadow of hope for the ungodly in that day.

*V*21: The religious ceremonies and observances are a mere empty pretence, hated and despised by God. The ritual of their holy days, the burning of their incense, (a symbol of prayer), and all these similar activities were hateful and despicable to God.

*V*22: **The burnt offerings** symbolized dedication, but it was apparent that the people were acting a lie because in their lives they set God's law at nought.
**The meat offering** symbolized thanksgiving, but their lack of obedience evidenced ingratitude [see *John* 14.15].
**The peace offering** symbolized communion but their pre-occupation with the wrong things showed that they were not even desirous of working with God. Though they brought 'fat beasts' – the best of their cattle – the lavishness of the gift was

rendered worthless by the fact that it was born of waywardness, not devotion of heart.

*V*23: Their songs and hymns of praise held no meaning for God [*cf* 1 *Sam* 15.22] because they came from hearts which were not pure in God's sight.

*V*24: Note the **'but'**. Away with hypocrisy and self-deception! On with righteousness and 'holiness of truth' [*Eph* 4.24]! Worship in spirit and truth involves allegiance to God's standards and love and honesty towards fellow-men: it includes right behaviour [*cf Hos* 6.6; *Mic* 6.8].

*V*25-27: These verses are typical of the burden of the eighth century prophets [*Is* 1.11-18; *Hos* 6.6; *Mic* 6.6-8]. Elaboration of the forms of worship is no substitute for obedience of heart. Jesus also underlines this truth in *Matt* 5.23-24.

The verses are quoted by Stephen in *Acts* 7.42-43. Some scholars use *V*25 in an endeavour to prove that there was no ritual in the wilderness period and that all sections in the Pentateuch laying down sacrificial and ritual requirements belong to a later date than Moses. To do this is to undermine the whole authority of the Mosaic Law and is completely unwarranted.

*V*25: This verse may be taken to mean, 'Was there all this elaboration of sacrifice and ritual in the wilderness days?' The Divine grace and deliverance was in no way dependent upon such performances. Matthew Poole comments: 'Their fathers and they, though at so great distance of time, are one people, and so the prophet considers them in this place. *Have ye offered*? Did you not frequently omit to offer, and yet were not reproved or plagued for the omission, when your frequent removes, and many other difficulties, made it unpracticable? So little is sacrifice with your God. And yet, when you did offer, was it *to Me* only? or did you not sacrifice to idols and false gods, and provoked Me? Will-worship and idolatry have

[77]

been hereditary diseases in your generations; and it is well-known, too, that these idolaters fell in the wilderness and are made admonitions to you!' – In other words there had always been perverseness of heart and now it had come home to roost! Since from the beginning, the wilderness days, they had veered towards apostasy, they would taste the judgement of apostasy.

V26: The Moloch and Chiun of the AV would be more correctly rendered Sakkuth and Kewan, and are in all probability the names of Assyrian gods, the latter being the planet Saturn (hence the reference to star worship). Although they had not always worshipped the particular false deities here named they had always been prone to turn aside to the false gods of the nations round about.

V27: Since, then, Israel forsook the true God and venerated Assyrian idols, into Assyria (beyond Damascus) they would be taken as captives. The irony of Divine retribution! (Stephen names Babylon instead of Assyria, the Jews apparently using the two words as synonyms on occasion).

FOR MEDITATION
1. 'The Day of the Lord', [V18-20]. Have I realised that history is heading up to such a day? This final day of accountability? [Rom 14.12; 2 Cor 5.10]. What will it mean for me? Joy or mourning? Am I to be numbered with the wise or the foolish virgins? [Matt 25.1-13]. Oil was the distinguishing factor, and oil is often used in Scripture as the symbol of the Holy Spirit. Am I truly 'born of the Spirit'? Does He control my life? Remember 1 Cor 6.19-20. There will be only two sorts of people in that day. Look up Rom 2.6-10.
2. Forms of religion without true allegiance of heart expressed in behaviour are not merely empty, they border upon blasphemy! God cannot just ignore them: He hates them. God will not be pacified by man's offering. Only the blood of Christ can make peace with God. [Rom 3.24-25; Eph 2.13-14; 1 John 1.7, 2.1], Man

receives the proffered gift of forgiveness via repentance towards God and faith towards our Lord Jesus Christ [*Acts* 20.21].

3. The human heart is prone to turn away from God. As Robert Robinson put it, 'Prone to wander, Lord, I feel it . . . !' Inclination to idolatry exercises a tremendous sway in the human heart. We find it hard to put God first and to keep God first in our lives. Love of people or things is always seeking to possess our hearts and lives. We can never depend on our hearts, but only on what God has done and is doing in them [*Jer* 32.38-41; *Phil* 1.6].

4. The wages of sin [*V*27]. Sometimes we may be tempted to say that the pressure of discipleship is too much but we must consider well the alternative. Then study the promises in such verses as in *John* 8.12; 14.6; and 15.5. If I am a Christian I am compelled at last to own that I need a 'hiding place' and He alone can provide it. *Ps* 73.25-26 is true for me as well as for the Psalmist!

> *Thou art my Life, if Thou but turn away*
> *My life's a thousand deaths; Thou art my Way:*
> *Without Thee, Lord, I travel not, but stray.*
>
> FRANCIS QUARLES
> [Emblems, Book III, No 7]

## Chapter 6 *V*1-8

1 Woe to them that are at ease in Zion, and trust in the mountain of Samaria, which are named chief of the nations, to whom the house of Israel came!

2 Pass ye unto Calneh, and see; and from thence go ye to Hamath the great: then go down to Gath of the Philistines: be they better than these kingdoms? or their border greater than your border?

3 Ye that put far away the evil day, and cause the seat of violence to come near;

4 That lie upon beds of ivory, and stretch themselves upon their couches, and eat the lambs out of the flock, and the calves out of the midst of the stall;

5 That chant to the sound of the viol, and invent to themselves instruments of music, like David;

6 That drink wine in bowls, and anoint themselves with the chief ointments; but they are not grieved for the affliction of Joseph.
7 Therefore now shall they go captive with the first that go captive, and the banquet of them that stretched themselves shall be removed.
8 The Lord God hath sworn by himself, saith the Lord the God of hosts, I abhor the excellency of Jacob, and hate his palaces: therefore will I deliver up the city with all that is therein.

Here Amos gives a vivid picture of the upper classes, apparently dwelling at their luxurious ease. They are called to consider the fate of the surrounding nations. In what ways can Israel claim to be better? Why should they be exempt from judgement? The prophet foretells that their self-sufficiency and pride will be brought low. They have thoroughly earned the judgement soon to come upon them, for they have become completely immersed in pride, luxury and revelry, and have been utterly careless of the moral state of the nation. They have not grieved over 'the ruin of Joseph', that is to say, over the decline of the nation, its apostasy, and the threatenings of imminent judgement.

*V*1: Three aspects of their sins are declared in this verse –
1. **At ease in Zion** – careless materialism and thoughtless self-indulgence [*cf Deut* 8.10-18; *Is* 32.9].
2. **Trust in the moutain of Samaria** – security in their walled and defenced cities. These people have 'made flesh their arm' [*Jer* 17.5].
3. **Named chief of the nations** – this may be intended to demonstrate how they were 'giving themselves airs'. Instead of seeing their election by God as a ministry committed to them to bring others to the light, they thought of it as an indication of their national superiority. Alternatively, they

are reminded that this inheritance was not theirs by right but they had been brought into it by God. Their self-confident folly and ingratitude are both laid bare!

*V*2: They are directed to look at the proud cities which have already been brought low. What right have they to think themselves secure?

**Calneh** – A site approx 220 miles north of Damascus, between the Upper Euphrates and the Mediterranean Sea (near ancient Arpad). See D. J. Wiseman in *The New Bible Dictionary*.

**Hamath** – A fortress (or citadel) commanding the 'entering in of Hamath' [*Amos* 6.14] which led to the valley between the two great ranges of Lebanon. This valley was the main line of communication between Egypt, Palestine and Syria to the South, and Assyria and Babylonia to the North and East. Conquered by Jeroboam II, it was afterwards taken by the Assyrians whose acquisition of it would give Israel but little joy.

**Gath** – the chief of the Philistine cities which had been reduced by Uzziah [2 *Chron* 26.6], and earlier by Hazael, King of Syria [2 *Kings* 12.17].

*V*3: They were deceiving themselves by thinking that the day of danger was very far off. In fact the evils found in their midst, including 'acting violence against the poor' continually hastened its approach.

*V*4: **Beds of ivory** – the excavated ruins of Samaria have produced many evidences of the extensive use of ivory for decorative purposes, but in such a state as to indicate a violent overthrow of the city [*cf* 3.15].

**Stretch themselves upon their couches** – here we see the upper class reclining in idleness whilst the poor whom they have reduced to slavery labour in the fields.

**Eat the lambs . . . and calves** – they pick out the youngest and choicest of the flock as special delicacies for their own gratification, regardless alike of sound economics, care for the poor, or the service of God. Their only concern was self-gratification.

*V*5: **Idle songs** – Calvin remarks that they behaved as though they were continually at celebrations and festivals. They fancied themselves as being musically the equals of David but we may note that there was a marked contrast in the dedication of their talent. We are reminded of the saying of the wise, 'The heart of fools is in the house of mirth' [*Eccles* 7.4].

*V*6: Their drinking habits are marked by ostentation and extreme self-indulgence. They do not use cups but bowls. In pursuit of the same selfish objective they spend prodigally on the most expensive perfumes.

**They are not grieved for the affliction of Joseph** – in their pursuit of selfish pleasures and gratifications they are completely unmindful of the desperate need of the majority of their countrymen. Like the brothers of Joseph in previous days, they 'eat their bread' whilst their brethren languish in the pit.

*V*7: Briefly and pointedly their doom is threatened. The language here is deliberately terse in contrast to the description of their lavish banqueting.

*V*8: The empty pride and futile glorying of Israel will all be stripped away. The mighty luxurious city of Samaria will be delivered into captivity [*cf Is* 23.9, spoken of luxurious Tyre].

FOR MEDITATION
1. Am I carelessly at ease? Do I revel in a life of material plenty? Maybe I suffer from a spiritual version of this trouble? Perhaps I enjoy the luxury of being in a sound church and enjoy its fellowship and teaching? Am I careless of the needs of others at home or overseas? Is my religion nothing more than one of 'happy meetings'? Am I seeking to enjoy it without even realising my responsibility to Christ, His Church, or the lost?
2. The following extracts from Spurgeon on 'ease in Zion' are worthy

of note: 'Among those at ease in Zion (the Church) are certain careless folk: they belong to a very large family. You know how many we have, even amongst those who frequent our sanctuaries, who say "Begone, dull care". They never sit down for half an hour and turn over the Word of God to see whether these things (those preached to them) be so. "No! they say, let well alone" . . . Sometimes they venture to make a profession of religion. But you might hope to build a palace with pillars of smoke, or adorn a queen's brow with dewdrops, sooner than find any truth in their godliness. Their convictions are always superficial – a sort of scratching of the soil as with the old ploughs; but there is no sub-soil ploughing, no turning up and breaking the clods, no tearing up of the vitals of their consciences, no revelation of themselves to themselves . . . Woe unto you, woe unto you, if thus you are at ease in Zion!'

A century and a half ago a Suffolk clergyman who later became archbishop of Dublin was told by one of his parishioners that he did not think a person should go to church to be made uncomfortable. The minister replied that he thought so too, but whether it should be the sermon or the man's life that should be altered, so as to avoid the discomfort, must depend on whether the doctrine preached was right or wrong.

'A sinner for doing nothing' was the comment of one who had been awakened under a sermon from the words, 'Woe to them that are at ease in Zion'. It was a new thought to the man who had been comforting himself with the plea that he had done nothing very bad. But, under conviction, he saw that his greatest sin was the very thing in which he had been finding comfort, namely, that he was always and for ever 'doing nothing'.

3. It is possible for a Christian's songs of praise to be no better than 'idle songs' and for him to employ his religion as a kind of entertainment. Do I mean the hymns I sing? Am I seeking God's glory in my worship and soul winning, or do my religious exercises really have 'me' in the centre?

4. Does God get the best of my life? – Do I live in the spirit of 2 *Sam* 24.24? Or *Mal* 1.7-8, 3.8? Is God truly glorified in every aspect of my life – thought, action, work, play, home, school, church, and what have you? Am I concerned (to use a fine expression from one of the ancient fathers), 'to eat and drink and sleep eternal life?'

5. David devoted his talent for music to the service of God and to the ennobling of His worship. How do I use my gifts?

6. How much self-indulgence am I prepared to allow myself? Remember how the Son 'pleased not Himself'[*John* 6.38; *Rom* 15.3; *Heb* 5.8].

7. We must face the fact of the Divine judgement. The Lord has sworn by Himself. He can swear by no greater. His wrath is as sure as His grace. Compare *V*8 with *Heb* 6.13-20.


## Chapter 6 *V*9-14

9 **And it shall come to pass, if there remain ten men in one house, that they shall die.**

10 **And a man's uncle shall take him up, and he that burneth him, to bring out the bones out of the house, and shall say unto him that is by the sides of the house, Is there yet any with thee – and he shall say, No. Then shall he say, Hold thy tongue: for we may not make mention of the name of the Lord.**

11 **For, behold, the Lord commandeth, and he will smite the great house with breaches, and the little house with clefts.**

12 **Shall horses run upon the rock? will one plow there with oxen? for ye have turned judgement into gall, and the fruit of righteousness into hemlock:**

13 **Ye which rejoice in a thing of nought, which say, Have we not taken to us horns by our own strength?**

14 **But, behold, I will raise up against you a nation, O house of Israel, saith the Lord the God of hosts; and they shall afflict you from the entering in of Hemath unto the river of the wilderness.**

*V*9: Those not killed in war or taken into captivity would perish by pestilence. Amos is emphasizing the facts of future judgement already present in previous oracles.

*V*10: Even the kinsman who is preparing to do the ceremonial burnings to honour the dead [as in the case of King Asa: 2 *Chron* 16.14] will not dare to mention the Name of the Lord, so great will be his fear of the judgement which appears both terrifying and complete. Matthew Henry sees this as an expression of the foolishness of men which perverts their hearts, 'God is so angry with us that there is no speaking to Him: he is so extreme to mark what we do amiss that we dare not so much as make mention of His name.' Fausset in Jamieson, Fausset and Brown's commentary catches the pathos of these verses when he writes, 'The one survivor was sick, and in the remote corner of the house. None else was left. All, even the bodies, had now been removed. One alone remained of all the throng that once filled with sounds of merry-making the luxurious mansion. Even he is silenced, when he ventures to speak of God, as though hope from God is now utterly gone'. Remember *Matt* 10.28: there is a fear of God which is healthy: we must not become over-familiar. Our God is a consuming fire. [*Heb* 12.29].

*V*11: The judgement of God is without respect of persons: small and great alike will be dealt with according to their deserts.

*V*12: The so-called justice of the time had become poison and wormwood and the prophet warns that it is as senseless to pervert justice and expect Divine favour as it is to expect horses to run upon rocks or for oxen to plough upon rock. Calvin comments, 'Those that will not be tilled as fields shall be abandoned as rocks.'

*V*13: Some scholars suggest that a play on words is intended here:
**A thing of nought** – Lodebar: **horns** – Karnaim. These, they say, were the names of two of the cities taken from Syria by Jeroboam II. R S V favours this reading. The Berkeley version and many commentators prefer to take **Lodebar** and **Karnaim**

as common, not proper, names and translate – 'You rejoice in what is nothing; who say "Is it not by our own strength we have taken horns for ourselves".' Horns were a common symbol of power or authority and are probably intended to refer to the extensive conquests of Jeroboam II who captured Damascus and restored Israel's territory to the Sea of the Arabah (Elath). The application of these two words to two particular cities is only conjectural, not certain. Karnaim is not mentioned at all in Scripture (unless here) and Lodebar is not mentioned outside of 2 *Sam*. Hence if any reader looks for mention of these places in the records of the reign of Jeroboam II he will not find them.

The sense however is plain. The people were glorying in some temporary successes and were making them the basis of a foolish self-confidence, since their dangers were extremely great and their successes, by comparison, exceedingly small. How easily man takes credit to himself and makes some small achievement the basis of a similar foolish trust!

*V*14: Their own fancied strength would be very insignificant when they were confronted by the nation used as the instrument of the Divine judgement. God would raise up against them the Assyrians – not named by Amos – who would devastate the land from North to South.

FOR MEDITATION

1. Am I trying to plough upon rock by expecting God to bless my labours whilst I continue to harbour sin in my life?
2. I cannot successfully ignore the laws of spiritual harvest [*Rom* 2.6-10; *Gal* 6.6-8].
3. Am I prone to rejoice in 'a thing of nought'? This happens when I take hold of some small success and make of it the ground of boasting that I am somebody. The grounds of self-confidence are usually very slender. In their extreme form they lead to the boast, near blasphemous, but approved by some professed Christians – 'I am the master of my fate, I am the captain of my soul.' [*cf Jer* 2.13, 10.23, 17.5; *Rom* 7.18; 1 *Cor* 1.29-31].

4. Never lose sight of the fact that there is a 'Day of account' [*Rom* 14.12; *Heb* 9.27]. Do not be misled by the apparent delay in judgement [*Eccles* 8.11]; it is the result of Divine longsuffering.

5. We may summarize the lessons of verses 12-14 –

   (i) The failure to appreciate that whatever strength I have is by the grace of God.

   (ii) The futility of ploughing upon rock – I cannot defy God and prosper.

   (iii) The folly of human pride; we do some small thing and boast as though we had accomplished a mighty wonder.

   (v) The finality of the Divine judgement.

# 7: *Three Prophetic Visions*

Chapter 7 *V*1-3

1 Thus hath the Lord God shewed unto me; and, behold, he formed grasshoppers in the beginning of the shooting up of the latter growth, and lo, it was the latter growth after the king's mowings.

2 And it came to pass, that when they had made an end of eating the grass of the land, then I said, O Lord God, forgive, I beseech thee: by whom shall Jacob arise? for he is small.

3 The Lord repented for this? It shall not be, saith the Lord.

## THE DEVOURING LOCUSTS

*V*1: **Formed** – as a potter forms a vessel: indicates the creative power of God. **Grasshoppers.** The word rendered 'grasshoppers' in AV is generally agreed to be better rendered 'locusts'. The judgement of God is presented in terms of a locust plague. It may be that such a plague actually happened and the vision here speaks of reality and not of mere symbol.

The prospect of a splendid crop was blighted [*cf* 4.9]. The 'first mowings' went as exaction by the king to feed his horses, and these had been safely gathered. Then at the period of 'latter growth' – after the late rains of March and April – the locusts were fully grown and ready to devastate the land. The prophet gave himself to intercession and before the devastation was complete, the Lord withdrew His hand of wrath.

Some interpreters (for example, Calvin) take the vision symbolically. The locusts represent human foes who will pillage the land. The growth of the grass after the king's mowings may represent the revival of Israel's fortunes in the reign of Jeroboam II. A personal experience of the locusts – as mentioned in Joel who prophesied somewhat earlier than Amos – may well have provided the background to the use of this symbolism, which reflects the moderate corrective chastening of God.

$V2$: The prophet intercedes for the people and is heard.

$V3$: Amos declares that God had been pacified through his intercession and prayer. The people had generally regarded the threatenings of the prophet as idle talk, but the prophet here says that they had escaped thus far only because of earnest intercession.

'The Lord had at first resolved to destroy you, but yet He waits for you, and therefore suspends His extreme vengeance, that by His kindness He may allure you to Himself: and this has been done through my prayers: for though you think me to be adverse to you, as I am constrained daily to threaten you, and as a heavenly herald to denounce war on you, I yet feel compassion for you and wish you to be saved. There is therefore no reason for you to think that I am influenced by hatred or by cruelty when I address you with so much severity. This I do necessarily because of my office but I am still concerned and solicitous for your safety, and of this the Lord is witness.' [Calvin].

**Repent** – This does not mean that God changes His purpose, but it represents an accommodation by God to the measure of man's understanding. The lesson is that God's judgements are always tempered by mercy and forbearance – 'as soon as He lifts up His finger, we ought to regard it as owing to His mercy that we are not instantly reduced to nothing. When it so happens, it is as though He changed His purpose, or as though He withheld His hand.' [Calvin].

**By whom shall Jacob arise?** Israel's hope is in God alone. He has no other friend upon whom to depend.

**For he is small** – He has no power in himself to save himself.


FOR MEDITATION

1. God forewarns of all the dangers which will follow from rebellion and disobedience. They were warned of the larvae even before the locusts were full grown. We are made aware of the seeds of sin and their consequences long before their full fruition.

2. The importance of the intercession of the godly man. Do I interest myself in the plight of the lost as Amos did? Remember that they were rejecting him but he still continued to love and pray and pity. Is not this seen also in Christ? [*Luke* 23.34]

3. The virtual paradox of the attitude of the prophet. The vehement denunciation of the people's sin is coupled with an earnest concern that they should repent before they were called upon to reap what they had sown. A lesson here for the preacher of today!

4. The prayer of the prophet. In contrast to the boasting of the people [6.13], the prophet saw the true state of Jacob – poor, needy, and dependent. This is how we must see man in spite of all his boasted achievement [*Matt* 18.3]

5. The mercy of God [2 *Peter* 3.9]. God 'repented' – not that He changed His mind but that he changed His course of action. He withheld the fully deserved punishment. We have here the language of 'accommodation' reminding us that His ways are far higher than our ways [*Is* 55.8–9]. We need to be cut down to size and reminded that God has to talk to us in 'baby talk'. Our problems with revelation are often caused because we think of ourselves as full-grown when we are mere babes.

6. Whether an actual locust plague is intended or the language typifies the Assyrian invasion, the truth of the inevitability of the Divine judgement is not less emphatic.

4 Thus hath the Lord God shewed unto me: and, behold, the Lord God called to contend by fire, and it devoured the great deep, and did eat up a part.

5 Then said I, O Lord God, cease, I beseech thee: by whom shall Jacob arise? for he is small.

6 The Lord repented for this: This also shall not be, saith the Lord God.

## THE CONSUMING FIRE

The punishment symbolized here is more severe than that indicated by the locusts. The oracle opens with the statement that the Lord is contending with His people. Emphasized is the idea of His personal abhorrence of sin.

*V*4: It is the Lord, the covenant-keeping God, who is actually behind these judgements. They are not sent because He lacks love or power or interest in His people but because of these very characteristics. This second judgement is much more severe than the first. The locusts only consumed the grass, the fire will penetrate the very depths, but even so it will not be complete – 'it did eat up a part'.

**The great deep** – we are to understand this to refer to 'the water under the earth' as mentioned in the ten commandments [*Exod* 20.4], that is to say, the source of supply of 'fountains and depths that spring out of valleys and hills' [*Deut* 8.7].

*V*5: Once again the prophet intercedes, and we may note the brevity and pointedness of his intercession.

*V*6: Again the Lord stays the hand of judgement.

FOR MEDITATION
1. Failure to heed the warnings of God makes me doubly responsible and heaps judgement upon my head.
2. Failure to respond to the forbearance of God is yet more criminal [*Rom* 2.4-5].

3. The prophet continued to intercede. Have I learned love and patience after this fashion?
4. Many of the most effective heartfelt prayers of Scripture are very brief. I do not have to be long-winded in order to gain my suit with God! [*Matt* 6.7-8].
5. The greatness of the Divine forbearance and longsuffering, in refraining from striking, is striking.

## Chapter 7 *V* 7-9

**7 Thus he shewed me: and behold, the Lord stood upon a wall made by a plumbline, with a plumbline in his hand.**

**8 And the Lord said unto me, Amos, what seest thou? And I said, A plumbline. Then said the Lord, Behold, I will set a plumbline in the midst of my people Israel: I will not again pass by them any more:**

**9 And the high places of Isaac shall be desolate, and the sanctuaries of Israel shall be laid waste: and I will rise against the house of Jeroboam with the sword.**

## THE PLUMBLINE

This is the third and final vision of judgement. No longer is there any place for intercession and delay. Grace may not be abused for ever!

*V*7: The wall represents the kingdom of Israel and the plumbline the searching equity of the Divine judgement. The wall had been built carefully and checked by plumbline: so the nation of Israel had received the rule of the Divine law. As the wall could be expected to be straight so the nation could justly be tested by the Divine standards. The judgement was according to responsibility.

*V*8: No longer would God pass them by. This threat virtually excludes any further attempt by the prophet at intercession – compare Abraham pleading for righteous persons in Sodom

[*Gen* 18.23-33], and God's express command to Jeremiah [*Jer* 7.16, 11.14, 14.10-12]. God's 'dead-line' had been reached.

*V*9: **The high places.** These had become the centres of debased pagan worship. Some of them had at one time been places where God had revealed Himself [*eg* 1 *Kings* 3.4], but now they had become polluted by their association with heathendom. The phrase here, 'the high places of Isaac', is unusual. It may be a reference to the religious associations of Beersheba [*Gen* 26.23-25], which seems again to have become a prominent sanctuary [5.5], and in resorting to it the Israelites were claiming that they were truly heirs of Isaac, although in fact the religion they practised there was far from the truth of Jehovah.

**Sanctuaries** – Perhaps intended to emphasize the apostasy from the true sanctuary of Jerusalem. God had not yet abandoned the temple at Jerusalem in spite of the deviations from the truth that were practised there. In Judah, though not in Israel, monarchs appeared from time to time who engaged in genuine reformation; Asa, Jehoshaphat, Hezekiah, and Josiah are all notable in this respect.

**The sword** – As the rule of 'the house of Jeroboam' ended a score or more years before the Assyrian invasion of Israel, the term may be prophetic of the fate of the royal house, for Zechariah, Jeroboam's son, reigned only six months before being assassinated by Shallum the son of Jabesh [2 *Kings* 15.10]

FOR MEDITATION
1. The plumbline reminds us of the equity of the Divine judgements wherever and whenever they fall. This is an important thing to remember when the wicked seem to triumph or we feel to be suffering unfairly. The ways of the Lord are equal [*Ps* 96.13; 98.9; *Ezek* 18.25]. The Lord Jesus Christ is the One to whom all judgement has been committed [*Acts* 17.31], so we have no cause to fear or fret since He is our Saviour and Lord. Remember *John* 10.27-29.

2. The imagery of the wall, carefully checked in building by the use of a plumbline, reminds us:
   (i) that God's kingdom is thoughtfully and carefully constructed. Each individual stone has been specifically chosen and prepared by God and each has a part to play [1 *Peter* 2.4-5].
   (ii) that God has given the plumbline of His law to His people so that they may be conformed to His image, and show themselves to be 'the servants of righteousness' [*Rom* 6.18].
3. The futility of an empty religious institutionalism is underlined again in 7.9. Men are not saved by form or creed but by personal relationship with the Lord through faith.
4. Various lessons on judgement are implicit here:
   (i) The equity of it.
   (ii) The inevitability of it.
   (iii) The terror of it.
   (iv) The careful detail of it.
5. We again refer to *Num* 32.23. There is only one place of refuge from sin [*Acts* 4.12]:

> *Tis there I would always abide,*
> *And never a moment depart,*
> *Concealed in the cleft of Thy side.*
> *Eternally held in Thy heart.*
>
> C. WESLEY

# 8: *Amaziah the Priest of Bethel Contends Against the Prophet Amos*

Chapter 7 *V*10–17

10 Then Amaziah the priest of Bethel sent to Jeroboam king of Israel, saying, Amos hath conspired against thee in the midst of the house of Israel: the land is not able to bear all his words.

11 For thus Amos saith, Jeroboam shall die by the sword, and Israel shall surely be led away captive out of their own land.

12 Also Amaziah said unto Amos, O thou seer, go, flee thee away into the land of Judah, and there eat bread, and prophesy there:

13 But prophesy not again any more at Bethel: for it is the king's chapel, and it is the king's court.

14 Then answered Amos, and said to Amaziah, I was no prophet, neither was I a prophet's son; but I was an herdman, and a gatherer of sycomore fruit:

15 And the Lord took me as I followed the flock, and the Lord said unto me, Go, prophesy unto my people Israel.

16 Now therefore hear thou the word of the Lord: Thou sayest, Prophesy not against Israel, and drop not thy word against the house of Isaac.

17 Therefore thus saith the Lord; Thy wife shall be an harlot in the city, and thy sons and thy daughters shall fall by the sword, and thy land shall be divided by

line; and thou shalt die in a polluted land: and Israel shall surely go into captivity forth of his land.

*V*10: The priest initiated the 'persecution' of Amos. We may compare the experience of Jeremiah and remember how men with a vested interest in religion have tried to silence the true spokesman of God. Jesus Christ Himself is the supreme example, followed by many of the great leaders of Reformation – Wycliffe, Huss, Tyndale, Luther. Amos is accused by Amaziah of subversive activities [cf *Jer* 26.8-11; *Luke* 23.2]. We may find our loyalty to Christ coming into conflict with every love and loyalty. Are we really ready to put Him first?

**The land is not able to bear his words** – the Word of God 'cuts' [*Heb* 4.12]. Compare the impact of Elijah [1 *Kings* 18.17]. Jeremiah speaks of the devastating impact of the word of God and likens it to a fire and a hammer [*Jer* 23.29].

*V*11: Amos had not actually said that Jeroboam would die. In 7.9 he had announced the downfall of the house of Jeroboam, and in 5.27 he had foretold the national captivity. Maybe Amaziah deliberately perverted the word of the prophet in this way to engage the personal wrath of the king.

*V*12: 'Get off back to your own land', cried Amaziah. That was how much the message of the prophet was appreciated! To be the spokesman of God often means that you get but little thanks, no thanks at all or lively opposition.

**Go, flee thee away.** This makes clear that his life was in real danger if he stayed in the North.

**Eat bread** – suggesting that Judah would be a place of security where he might prophesy evil to his heart's content.

*V*13: RSV 'But never again prophesy at Bethel, for it is the king's sanctuary and it is a temple of the kingdom.' Maybe here, perhaps unwittingly, Amaziah was emphasizing the height of the rebellion of the Northern Kingdom. Bethel was the king's 'chapel' by royal rather than Divine appointment:

in the same way it was the national sanctuary set up on the basis of political expediency, and certainly not by the appointment of God.

The warning here was very pointed and direct, reinforced with a very suggestive hint that Amos would be well advised to seek easier fields of service. Paul speaks of Satan as transforming himself into an angel of light [2 *Cor* 11.14] and here we have an instance of the wiliness of Satan, for the suggestion Amaziah made must have had a strong appeal to Amos at the purely human level.

*V*14: Amos answers Amaziah, showing how he was not free to follow the priest's counsel. He had been sent by God and consequently had no mandate to choose his own field of service.

**I was no prophet, neither was I a prophet's son.** The prophet was no religious professional who had been nurtured in one of the prophetic schools, but a countryman, called from a very lowly station in life.

*V*15: **But** he had experienced an unmistakable call of God. He puts it very simply – 'the Lord took me'. There was an irresistible power about the Divine call [*cf Jer* 1.4-10; 1 *Cor* 9.16]. This does not mean that the prophet went against his will, but that he went by constraint!

**As I followed the flock.** Amos was faithfully pursuing his calling when the Lord took him. The man who cannot perform small tasks faithfully is not fitted to take charge of greater matters [1 *Tim* 3.4-5]. The call of God came to Moses whilst he was minding sheep and to Elisha as he was following the plough.

**Go, prophesy.** The command was simple and clear. Since Amos had no professional qualifications or training, he could do nothing but lean on the Divine sufficiency.

*V*16: Amaziah was telling Amos not to do the very thing

which God had commanded to be done – so different are the ways of God and of false prophets!

*V*17: The nature of this judgement is reminiscent of Deuteronomy 28.30,32. Because Amaziah had so deliberately set himself against the revealed will of God, a very dreadful price will be exacted for his sin. Notice how sin involves others, particularly our loved ones.

**A harlot.** Violated by invading soldiers.

**Sons and daughters shall fall by the sword.** The members of his own family would experience the very judgement which he was saying would never take place. We see here the awful responsibility of the watchman who fails to do his duty. The man who is supposed to be the mouthpiece of God but who perverts his calling and resists the word of truth is faced with the terrible threat of reprobation.

FOR MEDITATION

1. If I stand loyal to the Word of God, I may expect to come into conflict with vested interests in the realm of religion. I must beware of becoming identified with them. I must continually test my motives and actions by the Word of God [*Ps* 139.23–24].
2. Am I ready to follow Christ, whatever other loyalty I may have to discard on the way? [*Luke* 14.26].
3. Does the Word of God pierce heart and conscience as I study? as I preach? [*Acts* 2,37, 7.54]. The Word of God has not changed, nor has the power of the Holy Spirit.
4. When the voice of 'little faith' whispers, 'Things are getting hot here and you could find a much easier sphere where people would appreciate you more!', would I be glad to listen, or would I hold fast to my divine commission?
5. Am I in the Church, in the place of His appointment, or is it the 'king's Chapel', I being the king?
6. Have I heard the call of God? If I am not preaching by Divine appointment, I should not be preaching! If I am not preaching, and the Lord is calling me to do so, had I not better respond at once? [*Matt* 21.28–31]. He will enable.
7. Does my faithfulness in the place where I am give any warrant for

the Lord's call to greater service? Have I realized that the Lord must find me faithful in few things before He makes me ruler over many things? [*Matt* 25.21].

8. Am I, like Amaziah, trying to silence the Word of God for personal ends? Perhaps I am shirking listening to the Word preached, and reading it carelessly or not at all, because it is making demands I am not willing to answer. If so, I must heed the fate of Amaziah. In such paths are the ways of death.

9. I must guard against being an unfaithful watchman. My unfaithfulness may bring disastrous consequences for others. The threatened judgements of God are as sure as His promised blessings.

> *His truth shall stand, His word prevail*
> *And not one jot or tittle fail!*

10. The Lord took me. Here is the guarantee of success. As when the Spirit of the Lord took possession of Gideon [*Jud* 6.34] the frailty of man is clothed with the invincible Divine strength.

# 9: *The Vision of a Basket of Summer Fruit*

**Chapter 8 *V*1-3**

1 Thus hath the Lord God shewed unto me: and behold a basket of summer fruit.

2 And he said, Amos, what seest thou? And I said, A basket of summer fruit. Then said the Lord unto me, The end is come upon my people of Israel; I will not again pass by them any more.

3 And the songs of the temple shall be howlings in that day, saith the Lord God: there shall be many dead bodies in every place; they shall cast them forth with silence:

The force of the oracle in the Hebrew consists [as in 6.13] in a play on words. The word for 'summer fruit' is **Qayits,** the word for 'end' is **Qets.** [*cf Jer* 1.11-12, where 'almond tree' and 'hasten' are almost identical words].

*V*1: **A basket of summer fruit.** The imagery is of fruit fully ripe which needs to be gathered at once.

*V*2: As the fruit demands instant attention so the sin of Israel demands the immediate attention of God in judgement [*cf Gen* 6.13]. The symbolism of the vision is made clear by the express word of the Lord. Note the repetition from 7.8.

*V*3: **Songs of the temple.** The songs of worship become

cries of mourning and these, along with the dead bodies scattered in the streets, will be the evidence of the fulfilment of the Divine threats. Cries of pain, howls of agony and then the silence of death!

FOR MEDITATION

1. The Lord showed unto me . . . and He said 'Amos what seest thou?' Do I see the things the Lord God would show to me? As I read His Word I need to pray continually, 'Open thou my eyes that I may behold wondrous things out of Thy law' [Ps 119.18] and as I live day by day, to remember with expectancy the promise 'I will instruct you and teach you the way you should go. I will guide you with mine eye' [Ps 32.8].

2. Summer fruit should remind us that God deals with us as His vineyard and expects fruit. Read Is 5.1-7 and John 15.1-2. What of my present fruitfulness? This would be a good time to read again Gal 5.22-23 and 2 Peter 1.3-11.

3. We should recall much more than we do, the grace which makes fruitfulness possible in the believer. The love which redeems us is a love which makes ample provision –

> His providences which speak of continual watchful care.
> His precepts which are the landmarks to show the way.
> His promises which encourage and lift us up.
> His patience which will never let us go.

4. Am I prepared for that day of spiritual harvest when final accounts must be rendered? The Lord Jesus Christ makes the reality of that day very clear [Matt 13. 41-42].

5. What will be the quality of my summer fruit:
   (i) full, ripe and sweet?
   (ii) decayed and corrupt?

6. Will the songs that I now sing become 'howlings' in the day of visitation [V3] or will they swell into the 'new song' which the people of God sing before the eternal throne? [see Rev 5.9-10]

7. Let me remember that in the time of judgement the 'much people in heaven' say 'Alleluia . . . for true and righteous are His judgements'. And again they say, 'Alleluia' [Rev 19.1-3].

# 10: *A Message of Judgement*

Chapter 8 *V*4-14

4 Hear this, O ye that swallow up the needy, even to make the poor of the land to fail,

5 Saying, When will the new moon be gone, that we may sell corn? and the Sabbath, that we may set forth wheat, making the ephah small, and the shekel great, and falsifying the balances by deceit?

6 That we may buy the poor for silver, and the needy for a pair of shoes; yea, and sell the refuse of the wheat?

7 The Lord hath sworn by the excellency of Jacob, Surely I will never forget any of their works.

8 Shall not the land tremble for this, and every one mourn that dwelleth therein? and it shall rise up wholly as a flood; and it shall be cast out and drowned, as by the flood of Egypt.

9 And it shall come to pass in that day, saith the Lord God, that I will cause the sun to go down at noon, and I will darken the earth in the clear day.

10 And I will turn your feasts into mourning, and all your songs into lamentations; and I will bring up sackcloth upon all loins, and baldness upon every head; and I will make it as the mourning of an only son, and the end thereof as a bitter day.

11 Behold, the days come, saith the Lord God, that I

will send a famine in the land, not a famine of bread
nor a thirst for water, but of hearing the words of
the Lord:

12 And they shall wander from sea to sea, and from the
north even to the east, they shall run to and fro to
seek the word of the Lord, and shall not find it.

13 In that day shall the fair virgins and young men faint
for thirst.

14 They that swear by the sin of Samaria, and say, Thy
god, O Dan, liveth; and, The manner of Beersheba
liveth; even they shall fall and never rise up again.

Here is a further oracle of judgement against the ungodly
rich.

*V4*: The particular objects of the denunciations here are the
wealthy who are again accused of the oppression of the poor.
**Ye that swallow up the needy.** Because of their profiteering
they had first of all swallowed up the poor man's land, forcing
him to sell out to them; then they swallowed the man himself
as he was compelled to sell himself into slavery. This attitude
was clean contrary to the spirit and precept of the law of
Moses.

*V5*: The prophet goes on to enlarge on other aspects of their
sin.

1. **Saying, when will the new moon be gone . . . and the
   Sabbath . . . ;** Even during the holy days they were rest-
   lessly waiting for the earliest possible moment to engage
   again in their dishonest trading and acts of oppression.
2. **'Making the ephah small and the shekel great . . .';** they
   were giving short weight and demanding high prices.
3. **Falsifying the balances by deceit . . .;** they engaged in a
   third deliberate conspiracy to defraud others, adjusting the
   scales by which money and goods were weighed, to the
   customer's disadvantage [cf Deut 25.13-15; Prov 20.10].

[103]

Such was their avarice that they would engage in any low dishonest practice to make profit.

*V*6: Not only do they enslave the poor but they give them a very poor return for their enforced servitude – a single piece of silver or a pair of shoes. Then in return for their hard-earned cash they sell them the refuse of the wheat. In a similar passage, Isaiah denounces them for grinding the faces of the poor [*Is* 3.14-15].

*V*7: The Lord will not forget this. He swears to this effect 'by the excellency of Jacob', that is, by His own Name. Alternatively, as Calvin suggests, it may mean by the spiritual privileges of Israel, the adoption of Israel as His own peculiar people. Just as His promises of grace are confirmed by oath, so are His threats of judgement.

*V*8: The land which at the moment seems so secure will tremble; it will be shaken to its very foundations.
**Flood** – RSV reads 'Nile'. The Berkeley version translates the verse 'All of it shall rise like the Nile and it shall be tossed and sink like the river of Egypt'. The Hebrew **Yeor** means 'flood' and doubtless the annual flooding of the Nile is meant. The idea is one of utter instability and calamity [*cf Dan* 9.26]. **Cast out and drowned.** Here is a land utterly overwhelmed.

*V*9: The 15th June, 763 BC was the date of a solar eclipse, visible as a partial eclipse in Israel. Amos uses this as a material symbol of deep sorrow and tragedy [*cf Jer* 15.9; *Ezek* 32.7-10; *Matt* 27.45].

*V*10: The deep mourning of the whole nation is now portrayed. The festivities will be turned into times of mourning, the idle songs into heartfelt lamentations. Fine clothes will give place to sackcloth; heads will be made bald; both things being signs of grief and sorrow. The bitterness of those days for the nation will be like the mourning for the death of an only son [*cf Zech* 12.10].

*V*11: Those who would not hear the Word of the Lord will now experience the loss of it. They did not appreciate its presence with them as it was spoken by the prophets; they will now learn its value by the withdrawal of it. This is the most disastrous thing which can befall a nation.

1. No Divine law to regulate its life.
2. No calling to repentance and spiritual and moral purity.
3. No promises to encourage and sustain.

Though men do not realize it, this is tragedy indeed, for when the Word is withdrawn men both lose hope and cast off restraint.

*V*12: Too late men realize what they have lost [*cf Ezek* 7.26]. Though they now seek for it they do not find it [*cf Matt* 25.10-13]. God is sovereign as to when and to whom He offers His Word: we cannot afford to neglect it [2 *Cor* 6.2; *Heb* 2.1-3].

*V*13: In that day even the young and strong will faint [*Is* 40.30-31]. They will be left without hope, having rejected the only source of power which can enable them to stand.

*V*14: The idolaters will be utterly overthrown.

**The sin of Samaria** – 'the guilt of Samaria' [Berkeley version]. Commentators suggest that this refers to the calves of gold, at Bethel in the South and Dan in the North of the Northern Kingdom.

**Dan** – the chief shrine in the North of the Northern Kingdom.

**Beersheba** – The chief shrine in the South of Judah, previously mentioned in 5.5. Mohammedans still swear by the 'sacred way to Mecca'. 'As the way of Beersheba lives' [RSV].

FOR MEDITATION
1. Remember the concern of Christ for the poor and His very solemn warnings against the love of wealth [*Luke* 12.15ff, 16. 19-31,

18.18-27]. I must watch my own heart [*Matt* 6.19-21] and remember that I have an active responsibility to meet human need in Christ's Name [*Matt* 25.40; *Jas* 2.14-16].

2. God hates social injustice and oppression. In my dealing with others I must be pledged to absolute honesty ennobled by mercy.

3. How do I spend the Lord's Day? Perhaps I am not like the people denounced here, planning some new swindle; but is my heart obsessed with material and personal considerations? or is it well-pleasing to God?

4. The things God does and does not forget.

He will not forget the sins of the unrepentant [*Amos* 8.7].

He does not forget the cry of the afflicted [*Ps* 9.12].

He does not forget 'His own' [*Is* 49.15].

He will not remember the sins of the saved [*Jer* 31.34].

He will remember His Covenant [*Ezek* 16.60].

May we be kept from forgetting Him! [*Deut* 15.15; *Heb* 2.1-3]

5. Contrast the instability of this changing world order with the changelessness of God [*Heb* 1.11-12]. He can shake it at any time [*Hag* 2.6] but nothing can ever shake His throne. [*Ps* 2].

6. Keep in mind the importance of God's Word. If you neglect it, He may withdraw it. Failure to use it may cause us to lose it. It is likened to a sword [*Eph* 6.17], a fire, a hammer [*Jer* 23.29], all useful things in their way, but they have to be properly used. The benefits of the Word of God are briefly described in *Ps* 19.7-10, and displayed at length in *Ps* 119. There is in this Word 'A promise to be appropriated' [*Prov* 6.22] and an affirmation I should be able to make [*Jer* 15.16].

7. In the Lord alone is there strength for the day [*Deut* 33.25; *Is* 40.28-31].

# 11: *The Vision of the Altar*

Chapter 9 *V*1-8

1 I saw the Lord standing upon the altar: and he said,
Smite the lintel of the door, that the posts may shake:
and cut them in the head, all of them; and I will slay
the last of them with the sword: he that fleeth of them
shall not flee away, and he that escapeth of them shall
not be delivered.

2 Though they dig into hell, thence shall mine hand
take them; though they climb up to heaven, thence
will I bring them down:

3 And though they hide themselves in the top of Carmel,
I will search and take them out thence; and though
they be hid from my sight in the bottom of the sea,
thence will I command the serpent, and he shall bite
them:

4 And though they go into captivity before their
enemies, thence will I command the sword, and it
shall slay them: and I will set mine eyes upon them for
evil, and not for good.

5 And the Lord God of hosts is he that toucheth the
land, and it shall melt, and all that dwell therein shall
mourn: and it shall rise up wholly like a flood; and
shall be drowned, as by the flood of Egypt.

6 It is he that buildeth his stories in the heaven, and hath
founded his troop in the earth; he that calleth for the

waters of the sea, and poureth them out upon the face of the earth: The Lord is his name.

7 Are ye not as children of the Ethiopians unto me, O children of Israel? saith the Lord. Have not I brought up Israel out of the land of Egypt? and the Philistines from Caphtor, and the Syrians from Kir?

8 Behold, the eyes of the Lord God are upon the sinful kingdom, and I will destroy it from off the face of the earth; saving that I will not utterly destroy the house of Jacob, saith the Lord.

In this vision yet again, but using different imagery, the Lord reaffirms the inevitability of the judgement to come.

*V*1: **Lintel** – Capitals is a better translation and is given by RSV and the Berkeley version. It refers to the ornamental columns supporting the roof of the shrine.

**Posts** – rather 'thresholds' as in *Is* 6.4. Lange suggests 'foundation beams.' The mighty blows will shatter the columns, causing the very foundations to shake, and bringing down the ruins on the heads of the idolatrous worshippers and destroying them.

There is no archaeological evidence that there ever was a temple at Bethel. Some commentators have suggested that the 'altar' in 9.1 is only a symbolic reference. But there are two other possibilities. The Lord is seen standing beside the altar. Calvin argues that this must be the true shrine of Jerusalem since He would not deign to appear at any idolatrous shrine. But other commentators suggest that the reference is to the idolatrous shrine in Bethel which is now to be completely shattered. An earlier prophecy concerning this shrine is found in 1 *Kings* 13.1-5. For more than 150 years the warning note had been sounded again and again, only to be ignored by the Northern Kingdom. Now at last the day of inescapable reckoning is at hand. The completeness of the disaster is underlined in the last part of the verse. As there is no slipping through His fingers in salvation [*John* 10.27-29] so there is no escaping from His judgement.

*V*2: The transcendence of God is set forth here as in *Ps* 139.8. Though men dig down to hell they will not escape from Him since He is all-seeing and omnipresent as well as infinite in power. What a tremendous assurance for the believer! As surely as the Lord has the believer in His protection, so He has His hand on the perverse rebel. He will not suffer the one to fall or the other to escape!

*V*3: The same theme is emphasized again with different symbolism – the top of Carmel and the bottom of the sea. Mount Carmel was honeycombed with deep caverns which provided well-concealed places of refuge.

*V*4: Even surrender to their foes will not alleviate their fate. Grace persistently abused issues in implacable wrath. For so long God had watched over them with tender yearning love, but since His grace and long-suffering had been abused continually, God now swears 'I will set mine eyes upon them for evil and not for good.'

*V*5: Compare 8.8. The land will be overwhelmed by the judgement of God.

*V*6: **Stories** – upper chambers: **Troop** – vault. The Lord God is master of the heights and depths. He stretched out the heavens, He built the earth, He called for the waters of the sea and poured them out. Thus in brief but graphic language Amos expresses his faith in God as the Creator. In *Exod* 12.22 the Hebrew word here translated 'troop' is used of a **bunch** of hyssop (bound together). In 2 *Sam* 2.25 it is used of a **band** of warriors. Some commentators understand the term as used by Amos to refer to 'all animate creatures which are God's host' (He is the

[109]

Lord of hosts), but it seems best to understand it to refer to the vault of heaven.

*V*7: The Lord makes clear to them that whatever they think they are, they are no more by creation than any other people [1 *Cor* 4.7]. The Lord is clearly seen as the Ruler of History. He is the Lord behind all its great movements and migrations – Israel from Egypt, Philistines from Caphtor (probably Crete), Syrians from Kir [see note on 1.5].

*V*8: Now at last after long patience and forbearance the time of judgement will no longer be restrained. Even so, for the sake of His sovereign love, and covenant mercy, He will not utterly destroy the house of Jacob. A remnant is to be spared [*cf Is* 6.9-13; *Jer* 30.11, 31.36; *Rom* 11.25-29].

FOR MEDITATION
1. False religion will not be indulged for ever. It is vital that I know myself to be walking in the truth, or if not, that I seek the Lord while He may be found, and call upon Him while He is near [*Is* 55.6-7].
2. The Lord God is a consuming fire, able to shake the sanctuary, and not that only, but the very heavens and the earth. His wrath is a terrible matter: and not only is His wrath terrible, it is quite inescapable. The language of Amos is severe but it is reflected in the New Testament [*Heb* 10.29-31].
3. The Lord is omnipotent; He keeps the earth in equilibrium. Such an Almighty One is well able to keep His own people and bring sinners to judgement. This should encourage the believer to steadfastness.
4. The Lord is the absolute Lord of history. He has always been behind the great movements recorded in history and continues to rule for the safe home-coming of His elect until the great day of His triumphant appearing [*Matt* 24.30-31].
5. He is faithful to His covenant and will preserve a remnant in all safety through all the fires of implacable wrath. Our security rests in His unchanging grace.

6. Whatever blessings I enjoy are by His grace. I have nothing whereof to glory [1 *Cor* 4.7]. All things are 'of Him and through Him, and to Him; to whom be glory for ever' [see *Rom* 11.33-36]. Earth's foundations may shake, the earth may reel to and fro like a drunkard, its people may fall and rise not again – see *Is* 24.19-21 – but for ever blessed is the man who trusts in the Lord, and whose hope the Lord is [*Is* 26.3-4].

# 12: *A Promise of Restoration*

Chapter 9 V9-15

9 For lo, I will command, and I will sift the house of Israel among all nations, like as corn is sifted in a sieve, yet shall not the least grain fall upon the earth.

10 All the sinners of my people shall die by the sword, which say, the evil shall not overtake nor prevent us.

11 In that day will I raise up the tabernacle of David that is fallen, and close up the breaches thereof; and I will raise up his ruins, and I will build it as in the days of old:

12 That they may possess the remnant of Edom, and of all the heathen, which are called by my name, saith the Lord that doeth this.

13 Behold, the days come, saith the Lord, that the plowman shall overtake the reaper, and the treader of grapes him that soweth seed; and the mountains shall drop sweet wine, and all the hills shall melt.

14 And I will bring again the captivity of my people of Israel, and they shall build the waste cities, and inhabit them; and they shall plant vineyards, and drink the wine thereof; they shall also make gardens, and eat the fruit of them.

15 And I will plant them upon their land, and they shall no more be pulled up out of their land which I have given them, saith the Lord thy God.

Many critical scholars, without offering any strong objective reasons, have denied these verses to be original because they argue that the note of hope is not compatible with the rest of the prophecy. The Messianic promise of 9.11 is regarded as unsuitable to the context and omitted. Such an approach is pure subjectivism and may be categorically rejected. It is worth noting that this verse is used by James in *Acts* 15.16-17 as Messianic Scripture now fulfilled in the Christian Church and era. Actually Amos, as a prophet of God, is here seen to be in line with most of his fellow-prophets in ending his message with strong words of hope. Judgement on sin is most certainly his theme, but the rainbow of mercy is seen against the storm-cloud of wrath.

*V*9: Israel will be scattered among the nations as corn is shaken through a sieve, but not one true grain will be lost. Though the judgement will be universal in outreach it will be individual in discernment [*cf* 2 *Tim* 2.19].

*V*10: The sinners had long been boasting that the consequences of their sins would never overtake them [*Eccles* 8.11] but not one of them would escape. *All* unrepentant sinners will be destroyed.

*V*11: **In that day.** This day of dreadful judgement will also be a day of grace. A similar theme is found in *Jer* 30.9-11 and frequently in the New Testament, as in *John* 5.24-29 and *Rom* 2.6-10.

*V*12: **Edom** here probably stands as typical of all the enemies of God's people, since they had been the most inveterate of Israel's foes.

*V*11-12: The NT does not leave us in doubt as to the right understanding of these verses. James, at the Council in Jerusalem as described in *Acts* 15, quotes them (as found in the Septuagint Version) and throws light upon their interpretation.

He shows:

1. that the royal house of David would be brought into an extremely low condition before the fulfilment of the prophecy,
2. That the same royal house would be restored (a fulfilment only to be found in 'great David's greater Son'),
3. that this being accomplished, there would be seen among the 'residue' of men (represented by Edom, hitherto the enemy of Israel) a seeking after the Lord,
4. that the Lord Himself would accomplish this [cf Is 9.7: 'The zeal of the Lord of hosts will perform this'].

The general picture is one of restoration of Israel, followed by the ingathering of the Gentiles [cf Rom 11], and all this is to be brought about in and through the Messiah alone. 'The Lord God will give unto Him the throne of His father David, and He shall rule over the house of Jacob for ever, and of His kingdom there shall be no end' [Luke 1.32-33; see also Ps 2.8].

V13: The blessing promised in Lev 26.5 will now be fulfilled. Calvin remarks, 'The Spirit under these figurative expressions declares that the kingdom of Christ shall in every way be happy and blessed'. Such will be the abundance of the crop, that it can scarcely be fully harvested before the time for the next ploughing has arrived.

**All the hills shall melt.** ('dissolve themselves'). The vintage shall be so abundant that it will be as if the hills were dissolved in the streams of wine which flowed from them.

V14: The prosperity of the nation will be restored. Though this is not the place to open the subject at length, the New Testament does appear to teach that there may well be a considerable return of Israel to the Lord before the time of the end [cf Rom 11.15]. William Greenhill (1591–1671) in his Exposition of Ezekiel writes, 'There is a time when the Jews shall not only have mercy, but abundant and lasting mercy. God will gather them, pour out His Spirit upon them and

[114]

never hide His face from them any more. This time will be a happy and glorious time. For the house of Israel to be enriched with the gifts and graces of God's Spirit, which are excellent, and to have the light of God's countenance shining upon them, and that always, what can be more desirable? This condition as Paul says will be 'l fe from the dead' [*Rom* 11.15]. Now they are like dead trees without any sap in them, but then they will be like trees, well-rooted, full of sap, and in their greatest glory, full of branches, leaves, blossoms, fruit and the sun shining upon them' [*p* 774, Sherman edition].

**My people**. The ground of the restoring activity is the absolutely sovereign covenant love of God. He had made them His own, for His own name's sake. As Charles Wesley expresses it:

> *He hath loved, He hath loved us,*
> *Because He would love.*

**I will bring again.** The decision of His grace will be accomplished by His power. Here no mention is made of intermediary agents: He himself is personally and fully committed to the accomplishment of His work. He, the Good Shepherd, will bring the sheep back to the fold.

**The captivity**. A reminder of the hopelessness of their state, humanly considered. Apart from Divine intervention they were so many dry bones [*Ezek* 37].

**They shall build and inhabit.** Now by the grace of God they will work out the salvation which God had worked in them and for them. No longer will their attitude be one of rebellion but of glad co-operation: they will rejoice to work out that for which they have been wrought. Those once alienated will truly be made nigh [*Col* 1.21]; [*cf Jer* 32.38-40; 2 *Cor* 5.5; *Phil* 2.12].

**Vineyards, wine, gardens, fruit.** The imagery is of peace, cultivation, plenty, satisfaction and beauty. Now they are willing to bestow their labour whilst God is pouring out all the richness of full life to make labour fruitful [*cf Is* 35.1-2].

[115]

*V*15: The closing note is one which guarantees their secure enjoyment of blessing because it is the gift of God. They will never be dispossessed [cf *Is* 61.4-11; *Joel* 3.18-21]. The New Testament strikes the same joyful note throughout.

*Nothing shall the ransomed sever,*
*Nought divide them from the Lord.*

FOR MEDITATION

1. Once again we are reminded that for God's people even disaster has a beneficial purpose [*Rom* 8.28]. Certain assurance should result from this to enable us to face difficult days [see *Rom* 5.3-5; *Jas* 1.2-4; 1 *Peter* 4.17-19].

2. God intends us to be a holy people, therefore the sifting and purging are a necessary part of the purposes of grace [*Heb.* 12.6].

3. Not the least grain shall be lost. [*John* 10.27-29]. He will not allow me to be the first.

4. 'I will command and I will sift'. Hear Spurgeon on this verse: 'How easily the Divine purposes become facts! The Lord has but to command and His will is done. Omnipotence has servants everywhere. If those who serve Jehovah cheerfully shall not suffice to carry out His will, the very devils themselves, and the most rebellious of spirits, shall be chained to the chariot of His Divine decree and made to effect His designs.

*When God commands, who dare oppose,*
*Or ask Him why or what He does?'*

5. And again: 'Let us think of certain of the sieves in which you and I shall be tried. One is the *preaching of the Word*. Wherever the Gospel of Jesus Christ is faithfully preached, it acts as a discerner of spirits ... Every true preacher of the Gospel will be sure to become a spiritual detective. He may not know anything of his hearers, but in the course of his ministry he will speak as if he had entered into the very chambers of their heart, and read the secrets of their soul ... To many, plain preaching is very distasteful; they want to be patted on the back, and praised and extolled, and they like human nature lifted on high, and have sweet things said unto them ... but the

genuine Gospel, wherever it comes with power, in this respect acts like a sieve, for vain and foolish people are offended at that which searches and tries them, and so they fall to the ground with the chaff; while the precious wheat, under such a ministry, remains to the glory of God.'

6. The glory of the house of David is seen supremely in the triumph of Christ. As a Christian I have been adopted into that royal family, so my triumph is sure [2 Cor 2.14].

7. The glorious richness and fruitfulness of Christ's kingdom should be reproduced in me. Christ is the true Vine: believers are the branches: our Father in Heaven is the Husbandman: much fruit brings glory to Him [John 15.1-5].

8. The Lord is an expert at recovering captives. His grace guarantees that I shall be presented before Him at last, faultless and without blemish, so I am encouraged to build again the waste places of my life [cf Is 58.12, 61.4; Jer 31.15-17].

9. The power of Christ, the Prince of peace, will at last be demonstrated in the eternal security and triumphant glory of His people.

   Praise Him that the future is to be made radiant by His grace.

10.              *Oh, the joy to see Thee reigning,*
                 *Thee, my own beloved Lord!*
                 *Every tongue Thy name confessing;*
                 *Worship, honour, glory, blessing*
                 *Brought to Thee with one accord:*
                 *Thee, my Master and my Friend,*
                 *Vindicated and enthroned,*
                 *Unto earth's remotest end*
                 *Glorified, adored, and owned!*

                          F. R. HAVERGAL

# SOME OTHER
# BANNER OF TRUTH
# TITLES

# JONAH
## A Study in Compassion

*O. Palmer Robertson*

The Old Testament story catches the imagination and tells of a prophet who disobeys God and of a great fish which can swallow a man; it describes a city-wide revolt in a pagan country and a wonderfully-sighted prophet sulking in the sunshine. What does it mean?

In *Jonah: A Study in Compassion*, Dr O. Palmer Robertson's masterly knowledge of the Hebrew language, his vivid sense of the grace of God and the twisted state of a man's heart, and his ability to retell historical events and see their significance all combine to explain what the message of the book of Jonah really is, and—since there is a string in the tail—what it really means for us today.

*ISBN 0 85151 575 4*
*64pp. Paperback*

# ELIJAH

*A. W. Pink*

The life of Elijah has gripped the thought and imagination of preachers and writers in all ages. His sudden appearance out of complete obscurity, his dramatic interventions in the national history of Israel, his miracles, his departure from the earth in a chariot of fire all serve to that end. 'He comes in like a tempest, who went out like a whirlwind', says Bishop Hall; 'the first we hear from him is an oath and a threat'. Judgment and mercy were mingled throughout Elijah's astonishing career.

It is fitting that the lessons which may be drawn from Elijah's ministry should be presented afresh to our generation. History repeats itself. The wickedness and idolatry rampant in Ahab's reign live in our gross 20th century's profanities and corruptions. False prophets occupy large spheres of influence and truths dear to our evangelical forefathers have been downtrodden as the mire in the streets. A. W. Pink clearly felt called to the task of smiting the ungodliness of the age with the rod of God's anger while at the same time encouraging the faithful remnant. With these objects he undertakes the exposition of Elijah's ministry and applies it to the contemporary situation.

*ISBN 0 85151 041 8*
*320pp. Paperback*

# THE SOVEREIGNTY OF GOD

*A. W. Pink*

'Present day conditions', writes the author, call loudly for a new examination and new presentation of God's omnipotence, God's sufficiency, God's sovereignty. From every pulpit in the land it needs to be thundered forth that God still lives, that God still observes, that God still reigns. Faith is now in the crucible, it is being tested by fire, and there is no fixed and sufficient resting-place for the heart and mind but in *the Throne of God*. What is needed now, as never before, is a full, positive, constructive setting forth of the Godhood of God.

*ISBN 0 85151 133 3*
*160pp. Paperback*

# PROFITING FROM THE WORD

*A. W. Pink*

How much profit do we gain from our reading of the Bible? 'All Scripture', we are told in 2 Timothy 3:16, 17, 'is profitable'. But how much do we gain from our reading of Scripture, and by what means can we learn to profit more?

These questions, which are so fundamental to Christian experience and happiness, provide the theme for this book by Arthur Pink. Originally published as a series in *Studies in the Scriptures*, a monthly magazine edited by the author for over 30 years, it has all the characteristics which have, since the author's death in 1952, led to his recognition as one of the finest Christian writers of the twentieth century. Certainly the present book is among his best and will be a help to Christians both young and old.

*ISBN 0 85151 032 9*
*128pp. Paperback*

# THE THOUGHT OF GOD

*Maurice Roberts*

This is a collection of articles which have already been widely read and appreciated as editorials in *The Banner of Truth* magazine, of which Maurice Roberts is the editor. Pointedly biblical, they are thoughtful and searching, humbling and exalting, challenging and encouraging.

Like editorials in other journals, Maurice Roberts' articles have spoken to the needs of the times. But while many editorials appear to have only historical or sociological interest at a later date, in contrast these are of lasting value. They have God and his Word as their starting place; and their horizon stretches beyond time to eternity. Those who have already read them will rejoice to have these pieces conveniently and permanently in book form, while those who come to them for the first time will appreciate their freshness, relevance and power, and will find in them a seriousness which has a sanctifying effect on the heart and a clarifying influence on the spiritual vision.

*ISBN 0 85151 658 0*
*256pp. Paperback*

# COME DOWN, LORD!

*Roger Ellsworth*

*Come Down, Lord!* is a succinct, readable and biblically-based treatment of the vital theme of revival. Its seven short chapters go directly to the heart of the matter, as their headings indicate: We miss You; We need You; We wait for You; We will meet You; We have wronged You; We belong to You; We beseech You.

Taking as his starting place the widespread absence of the sense of God's holy presence and our need of his grace, Roger Ellsworth traces the profound analysis of the church's spiritual decay outlined in Isaiah 63:3-64:12, and applies its message to our times:

'We have heard for years that if we do not repent of our sins, God will send judgment upon us. We may think we are getting by with sin because things do not appear to be so bad. What most of us do not realize is God's judgment has already set in. Our apathy about spiritual things is God's judgment upon us.'

While calculated to expose our spiritual need, *Come Down, Lord!* will also stimulate repentance, prayer and fresh faith in the promised mercy of God.

*ISBN 0 85151 539 8*
*64pp. Paperback*

# IS THERE AN ANSWER?

*Roger Ellsworth*

Most people are vaguely aware of a man named Job who suffered incredible calamities. Few, however, realize how intensely relevant is the Old Testament book that bears his name. Job was asking the very questions many are asking today. It is true, of course, that others are not asking these questions. Their lives are bounded by pursuing material things and indulging themselves with a parade of pleasures. The only interest these people have in these questions is in devising ways studiously to avoid them. But for those who are weary of such a simplistic, superficial diet, this little work will have lasting value. These expositions will also be helpful to Christians who have struggled with these questions and are seeking to help others find answers.

*ISBN 0 85151 570 3*
*32pp. Booklet*

# WHAT'S WRONG WITH PREACHING TODAY?

*A.N. Martin*

The Christian church today stands in need of a recovery of good preaching. But how is that to take place? Part of the remedy lies in seeking to answer the question, What has gone wrong with preaching? The ability to analyse the weaknesses of contemporary preaching (and preachers) is essential to developing healthy and fruitful preaching.

In answering this vital question, Dr A. N. Martin draws on his own experience as a pastor and preacher and on the widespread opportunities he has had to teach and counsel other preachers. Fundamentally, however, his response is rooted in the biblical teaching on the character of those who preach and the message they are to proclaim. *What's Wrong With Preaching Today?* contains a searching message which will disturb complacency; but rather than create despair, it challenges all who preach (as well as those who hear) to rise to new levels of faithfulness and usefulness in the service of Christ.

*ISBN 0 85151 007 8*
*32pp. Booklet*